10 Minute Guide to
Lotus® 1-2-3® Release 3.4

Jeff Ott

alpha
books

A Division of Prentice Hall Computer Publishing
11711 North College Avenue, Carmel, Indiana 46032 USA

© 1993 by Alpha Books

International Standard Book Number: 1-56761-172-9
Library of Congress Catalog Card Number: 93-70026

Interpretation of the printing code: the rightmost number of the first series of numbers is the year of the book's printing; the rightmost number of the second series of numbers is the number of the book's printing. For example, a printing code of 93-1 shows that the first printing of the book occurred in 1993.

Publisher: *Marie Butler-Knight*
Associate Publisher: *Lisa A. Bucki*
Managing Editor: *Elizabeth Keaffaber*
Acquisitions Editor: *Stephen Poland*
Development Editor: *Seta Frantz*
Manuscript Editor: *Barry Childs-Helton*
Technical Support: *Kelly Oliver*
Cover Designer: *Dan Armstrong*
Designer: *Amy Peppler-Adams*
Indexer: *Jeanne Clark*
Production Team: *Tim Cox, Mark Enochs, Phil Kitchel, Tom Loveman, Michael J. Nolan, Carrie Roth, Barbara Webster*

Special thanks to C. Herbert Feltner for ensuring the technical accuracy of this book.

Screen reproductions in this book were created by means of the program Collage Plus from Inner Media, Inc., Hollis, NH.

Printed in the United States of America

Contents

Introduction

You've been hearing whispers about Lotus 1-2-3 Release 3.4, and how it helps people build spreadsheets to perform calculations and graphs for displaying numerical data. Now you're hearing that 1-2-3 does even more. It's time, you decide, to take action and learn about this software on your own! For 1-2-3 to meet your standards, you'll need:

- To know how to move around 1-2-3 efficiently and fast.

- To pinpoint which 1-2-3 features meet your needs, without spending hours lost in obscure manuals.

- To get clear instructions on basic program capabilities in plain English.

You have come to the right place: the *10 Minute Guide to Lotus 1-2-3 Release 3.4.*

What Is the 10 Minute Guide?

The 10 Minute Guide series is designed to help you learn new programs in a hurry, while keeping you on target. Through a series of lessons which take less than 10 minutes each, you can quickly master the basic skills needed to create impressive spreadsheets.

Conventions Used in This Book

The following icons help you find your way around the *10 Minute Guide to Lotus 1-2-3 Release 3.4.*

Timesaver Tips   These shortcuts will enhance your effectiveness as you use the program.

Plain English   These define new terms in everyday language.

Panic Buttons   These identify potential problems, and show you how to solve them.

 SmartIcons   These give you information about individual SmartIcons, and how to use them to boost your productivity.

For a look at some 1-2-3 features not covered fully in this guide, see the Table of Features, Table of Functions, and list of SmartIcons at the end of this book.

In addition to the icons listed here, the following conventions are also used:

`On-screen text`	Text that appears on-screen will be shown in computer font.
`What you type`	Information that appears on-screen when you type it will appear bold and in color, in computer font.

Items you select

Items to select from menus (or specific keys to press) will appear in color.

Menu names

The first letter is capitalized in the names of menus, commands, buttons, and dialog boxes. This will help you recognize them easily.

Release 3.4—What's New

Lotus 1-2-3 Release 3.4 offers powerful new enhancements that both the seasoned user and the beginner will appreciate:

- Simplified Install program.
- 1-2-3's SmartIcons, with the capability of creating and editing your own SmartIcons.
- 3-D graphs and other graph features.
- New Translate modules for use with Enable, MultiPlan, and SuperCalc 4.
- The ability to autoload worksheets when you start 1-2-3.

Trademarks

All terms mentioned in this book that are known to be trademarks or service marks are listed below. In addition, terms suspected of being trademarks or service marks have been appropriately capitalized. Alpha Books cannot attest to the accuracy of this information. Use of a term in this book should not be regarded as affecting the validity of any trademark or service mark.

Lotus and 1-2-3 are registered trademarks of Lotus Development Corporation.

Lesson 1

Starting
and Exiting
Lotus 1-2-3

In this lesson, you will learn how to start Lotus 1-2-3, turn Wysiwyg on and off, and exit 1-2-3.

The Lotus 1-2-3 program must be installed correctly on your hard disk before you can begin your work. (See the inside front cover for installation instructions.)

Starting 1-2-3

Follow these steps to start 1-2-3 from your hard disk:

1. Make sure you are at the DOS prompt where you installed 1-2-3. For example: C: or D:.

2. To move to the 1-2-3 Release 3.4 directory, where you installed 1-2-3 software, type CD\123R34 and press Enter.

3. Type 123 and press Enter. Briefly you will see a logo screen, showing the name and organization name you entered the first time you used Install. The work area appears on-screen next (Figure 1.1).

1

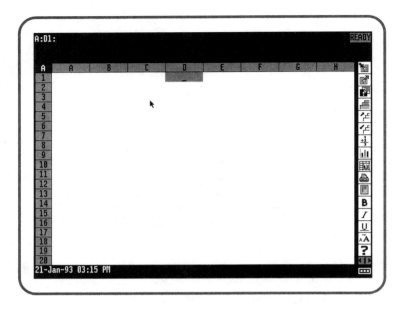

Figure 1.1 Lotus 1-2-3's initial work area.

It Won't Work If 1-2-3 presents start-up problems, an error message (such as Bad command or filename) will appear. Make sure you followed the "Starting 1-2-3" steps correctly; you could try these steps again. If they get you the same error message, try reinstalling 1-2-3, following the instructions on the inside front cover of this book.

Retrieving a File at Startup

You can retrieve a previously saved worksheet file at the same time you are starting 1-2-3, saving you several steps during a 1-2-3 work session. Here's how:

1. Type **123** and a space.

2. Type a - (hyphen) and the letter **w** (for worksheet).

3. Type the name of the file to retrieve.

4. Press Enter.

As an example, you would type **123 -wchecks** and press Enter to retrieve a file named CHECKS.WK3 in the 1-2-3 default directory.

Detailed Directions To retrieve a worksheet from a different drive or directory, type the complete path before the file name. For example, to retrieve CHECKS.WK3 from a disk in drive A, type **123 -wa:\checks** and then press Enter.

Alternate Start from Windows

You can start 1-2-3 from Windows if you've added the 1-2-3 icon to the Windows desktop. Refer to 1-2-3 documentation for the steps in creating an icon, or to Windows documentation for modifying the .PIF file.

Turning Wysiwyg On and Off

WYSIWYG (pronounced "wizzy-wig") stands for "What You See Is What You Get." Wysiwyg is also the name for one of 1-2-3's special programs. In this case, Wysiwyg lets you print exactly what you see on your screen. To demonstrate what it is and how useful it can be, we created the figures in this book with 1-2-3 in *Wysiwyg mode*. If you

3

have the right video card and monitor, Wysiwyg will start up automatically. Figure 1.1 shows the initial 1-2-3 display in Wysiwyg mode.

Follow these steps to remove or attach Wysiwyg. (Commands to attach Wysiwyg are in parenthesis.)

1. Press Alt+F10 to activate the Add-In menu (see Figure 1.2).

2. Use the arrow keys or the mouse to select Remove. (Select Load to add Wysiwyg.)

3. From the list of add-ins on-screen, select WYSIWYG . If you want to see additional choices, press → (the right arrow key).

4. Press Enter. (When loading, you will want to press Enter twice.)

5. Select Quit. 1-2-3 returns you to READY mode.

For more information on using Wysiwyg, see Lesson 19.

Exiting Lotus 1-2-3

Follow these instructions to end your work session and exit Lotus 1-2-3.

1. Press / (slash) or move the mouse pointer into the Control Panel (at the top of the screen) to display the 1-2-3 main menu. This menu, described in Lesson 3, contains commands you'll use as you work in 1-2-3.

2. Select Quit.

4

Shortcuts! 1-2-3 allows you to press the first letter of each command to select it (e.g., press Q for Quit, Y for Yes, etc.). You may also use the cursor arrows to highlight a command, and then press Enter.

3. Select Yes to end the session.

Add-In menu

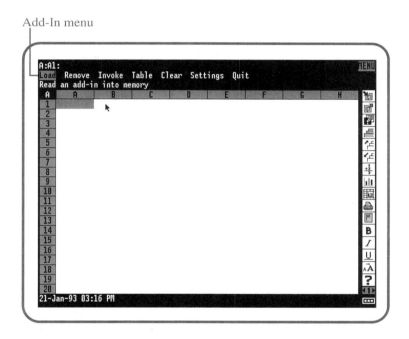

Figure 1.2 The Add-In menu.

1-2-3 returns you to the DOS prompt if you started 1-2-3 from DOS, or the Windows desktop if you started 1-2-3 from Windows.

5

It's Not a Bank!   If 1-2-3 asks you if you want to save a worksheet, it is because you have made some changes. For now, select No, and you can exit 1-2-3.

Details of saving a worksheet and exiting are given in Lesson 7.

In this lesson you learned how to start Lotus 1-2-3, turn Wysiwyg on and off, start from Windows, retrieve an application at start-up, and exit Lotus 1-2-3. In Lesson 2, you will learn about basic screen elements, and moving around 1-2-3 with the keyboard and mouse, should you choose to use one.

The Lotus 1-2-3 Screen

In this lesson you'll learn 1-2-3 basics, including the details of the work area, and how to use your keyboard or mouse to move around the worksheet.

Everything you need to work with 1-2-3—menus, commands, work area, and mode indicators—you will find ready and waiting on the 1-2-3 screen. All the elements are right there! Figure 2.1 shows a typical example. To display this screen, simply press the slash key (/). To see menu options that will display other such screens, move your mouse pointer (without clicking) into the menu area at the top of the screen.

1-2-3's Work Area

Have you ever kept books? Seriously? If so, you may have used some of the green columnar paper from an accountant's pad. 1-2-3's work area is organized into columns and rows, somewhat like the accounting paper. This arrangement (called a *worksheet*) makes it easy to organize your data. (Remember that columns "go" up and down, while rows "go" across the work area.)

Cells and Addresses

In all spreadsheet software, a *cell* is the basic unit of a worksheet; it allows you to store data, and always refers to the intersection of one *column* and one *row*. Figure 2.1 shows the spreadsheet cursor, called a cell pointer, located at the intersection of column D and row 12. The cell address is D12. When giving a cell address, refer to the column, in this case D, and then the row, in this instance 12.

How do you know which letters and numbers represent which columns and rows? Look at the top of 1-2-3's screen: a highlighted line segment tells you the column the cell pointer occupies. 1-2-3 boasts 256 columns, lettered from A to IV.

At the left edge of the work area is a line that numbers the worksheet's rows from 1 to 8192 (though of course they won't fit on your screen all at once). The highlighted segment locates your cell pointer by row. On your screen, you'll see cells A1 through H20. Later in this lesson, you'll learn how to move all around this work area.

The Control Panel

Look at the top of your 1-2-3 screen, and you'll see the *control panel* (see Figure 2.1). This is where you choose menus and commands to run 1-2-3. There are three lines on the control panel.

1. The first line of the control panel displays the current cell's:

   Address: A:D12 is the address, for instance, of the cell in worksheet A at the intersection of column D and row 12.

Format: If the cell is to be formatted in a way that differs from the default cell format, this choice controls the way 1-2-3 displays data in the cell.

Protection status: Lets you know whether you can make changes to the cell when worksheet protection is on.

Column width: If you have changed the default column width, this area shows the number of characters 1-2-3 will display in the cell.

Entry: This area shows the actual data stored in the cell.

Mode indicator: Located at the far right of the first line of the control panel, this tells you the *mode*, or state, in which 1-2-3 is currently running. (See Table 2.1.) After you press / (slash), for instance, 1-2-3 is in MENU mode and the mode indicator reads MENU.

2. The second line of the control panel shows you one of these three items:

   The current entry when you enter or edit data.

   The Main menu if you press / (slash) or < (the less-than symbol).

   The *prompts* (requests for information) that 1-2-3 needs to complete a command.

3. When 1-2-3 is in MENU mode, the third line of the control panel displays a description of the highlighted command, or a list of subcommands. When 1-2-3 is in FILES or NAMES mode, the third line shows a list of files or names.

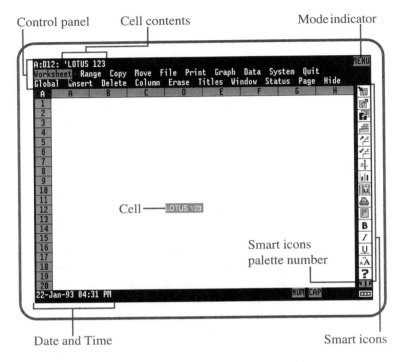

Figure 2.1   The control panel information.

1-2-3 uses the last line of the screen, the *status line*, to display the file and clock indicator, and various status indicators (such as CAPS when the Caps Lock key is on).

Mode Indicators

Whenever you are working with 1-2-3, mode indicators give you a message describing what's going on. For example, when you type a number or formula into a cell, the mode indicator VALUE appears in the upper right corner of the screen. 1-2-3's mode indicators are listed in Table 2.1.

10

Table 2.1 Mode indicators in 1-2-3 Release 3.4.

Mode	Description
EDIT	You're editing the contents of a cell.
ERROR	An error has resulted from a formula or operation; to remove this indicator, press Esc or Enter.
FILES	1-2-3 waits for you to select a file name.
FIND	1-2-3 is searching a database.
HELP	1-2-3 is displaying a Help screen.
LABEL	You are typing text (i.e., a *label*) into a cell.
MENU	1-2-3 shows you a menu, and waits for you to select an option.
NAMES	1-2-3 displays a list of range names, and waits for you to select one.
POINT	You are selecting some connected cells (a *range*).
READY	1-2-3 waits for you to give a command or enter data into a cell.
SETTINGS	You have called up a dialog box.
STAT	The current screen is a STATUS screen.
VALUE	You are typing a number (i.e., *value*) or a formula into a cell.
WAIT	Wait while 1-2-3 carries out a command.
WYSIWYG	1-2-3 is showing you what you'll get if you print.

Status Indicators

Status indicators let you know the type of operation 1-2-3 is performing. They also let you know when an error occurs, and the type of error it is. Table 2.2 shows the status indicators and what they are telling you.

Table 2.2   Status indicators in 1-2-3 Release 3.4.

Status	Description
CALC	Recalculate the worksheet.
CAP	The Caps Lock key is engaged.
CIRC	Correct a circular reference error (such as adding a total to a total).
CMD	A macro is running.
LEARN	1-2-3 is "learning" by recording a macro from your keystrokes.
END	You pressed End; press an arrow key to move the pointer.
FILE	You are in the process of moving between files.
GROUP	GROUP mode is in effect for this file.
MEM	Warning: your computer's memory is almost full.
NUM	The Num Lock key is engaged.
OVR	You are editing data in Overstrike mode.
PRT	1-2-3 is printing the current file.
RO	Read-Only; no changes to this file will be saved.
SCROLL	The Scroll Lock key is engaged.
STEP	A macro is running one step at a time.
ZOOM	You have a full-screen view of a worksheet window.

Removing Status Indicators   You can remove a status indicator by pressing Esc or Enter; you'll return to the READY mode.

Moving Around the Worksheet

Use the following pointer-movement keys to move around the worksheet.

Table 2.3   Using keys to move the pointer.

Press	To move cell pointer
← or →	Left or right one column.
↑ or ↓	Up or down one row.
Ctrl+← or Shift+Tab	Left one screen.
Ctrl+→ or Tab	Right one screen.
End, Home	To the bottom right corner of worksheet's active area.
Home	To cell A1, if column A is not hidden and worksheet titles are not set.
PgUp or PgDn	Up or down one screen.

You can also move around with a mouse as well as a keyboard. To use a mouse, you'll need to be familiar with these terms:

Point   Move the mouse so the pointer is over the cell or menu option you wish to select.

Click   When you point to the cell or option you want, press and release the left mouse button.

Drag   Put the mouse pointer at the point on-screen where you want your selection to begin. Press the left mouse button, hold it down, and move the mouse pointer until the group of cells you want is highlighted.

In this lesson, you learned about the 1-2-3 worksheet screen and how to move around in it. In the next lesson, you will learn how to use 1-2-3's menus and dialog boxes.

Lesson 3
Using 1-2-3's Menus

In this lesson you'll learn how to operate 1-2-3's menu system, select commands, retrieve a file, and get help.

The Main Menu

It's easy to gallop through 1-2-3. Simply select commands from the menus, and you're off!

Menu Selections   A *menu* is a series of choices that 1-2-3 displays in the second line of the control panel. You select a command from a menu by highlighting or typing the first character in the name.

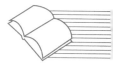

Table 3.1 lists Main menu commands, and a brief explanation of their purposes:

Table 3.1   Main menu commands in 1-2-3.

Command	Enables you to
Worksheet	Affect the whole worksheet.
Range	Select and work with a range of cells.

continues

Table 3.1 Continued.

Command	Enables you to
Copy	Copy a cell or range of cells.
Move	Move a cell or range of cells.
File	Perform various operations on files.
Print	Print a range of cells or a whole worksheet.
Graph	Create or change a graph.
Data	Work with database features.
System	Exit to DOS.
Quit	End the work session.

Selecting Menu Commands

When 1-2-3's Main menu first appears (see Figure 3.1), you'll see a list of the options available to you. *Commands* let you perform such tasks as copying data, saving files, and printing your worksheet. You make them work by selecting them from a menu.

The highlighted rectangle positioned on the Worksheet command is the *menu pointer*. Each time you move over a different command, the third line of the control panel displays either *subcommands* or information about the highlighted command.

To select a menu command from the menu with the keyboard:

1. Press the / (slash) key.

2. Use ← and → to move through the command list until the command you need is highlighted.

3. Press Enter.

Main menu   Main menu commands   Subcommands

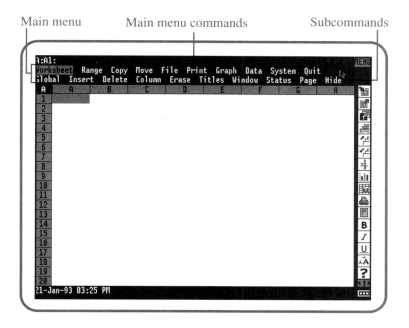

Figure 3.1   The 1-2-3 Main menu.

Alternate Selection   You can also select a command by pressing the first letter of its name on the keyboard.

The Right Slash   When bringing up the Main menu, be sure to use the / (slash) key, not the \ (backslash) key. If you made a mistake, return to the previous screen by pressing Esc, and press / (slash) to get the Main menu.

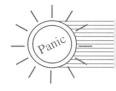

17

To select a command from the menu using the mouse:

1. Move the mouse pointer into the control panel area.

2. When the Main menu appears, click on the command you want.

Entering Information

Sometimes a command you've selected will require you to type information in order to continue. For example, if you choose /File Save from the Main menu, you'll be asked to enter the name of the file you are saving. In this case, type the path and the name of the worksheet. Don't put in an extension; 1-2-3 does that for you. Press Enter (or click the left mouse button), then press Esc repeatedly until you return to the Main menu.

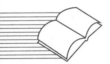

Leaving a Trail   Typing in a path tells 1-2-3 the drive and directory it should use to find your stored file. Your DOS manual can give you more details.

Dialog Boxes

Dialog boxes appear when Lotus needs more information about the function you are performing; they also display options available with the function. See Figure 3.2 for an example of a dialog box. To make a selection from a dialog box, follow these steps:

1. When a dialog box appears, press F2 to enter EDIT mode.

18

2. Press Tab to move to the option you want to edit, or press the first letter of the name of the option.

3. Using the arrow keys, highlight the option you want to edit.

4. Press the Spacebar to select the option.

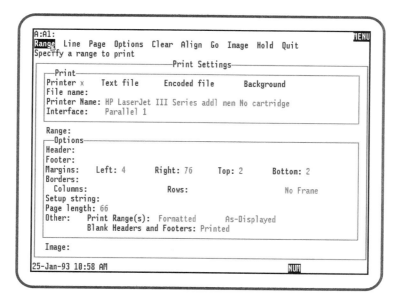

Figure 3.2   An example of a dialog box.

Help!

Press F1 (Help) at any time to see a Help screen of information about the part of the program you're using. When you press F1 (Help), the worksheet disappears temporarily, and a Help screen appears (see Figure 3.3). Notice

19

the words that appear in a contrasting color (or a brighter intensity) within the current Help screen, and at the bottom of the screen. These stand for related topics on which you can also get Help. To select one of them, use the pointer-movement keys to move to the topic you want, and press Enter. To exit Help, press the Esc key.

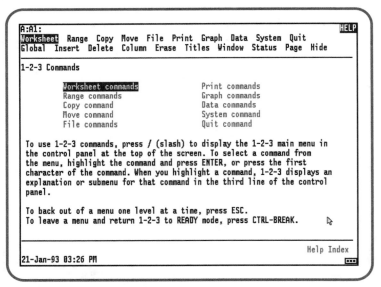

Figure 3.3 The 1-2-3 Help Index.

In this lesson, you learned how to access 1-2-3's Main menu, select menu commands, retrieve a file, and use the Help feature. In the next lesson, you will learn about using 1-2-3's SmartIcons to speed up routine operations.

Lesson 4
SmartIcons

This lesson shows you how you can perform routine steps quickly by using 1-2-3's SmartIcons.

Talk about making your spreadsheet look great! You can format a range of cells with a special font in the blink of an eye. Or you can bold and underline a heading with a click. How? With 1-2-3's SmartIcons.

SmartIcons are the sixteen buttons that appear at the far right of the worksheet, as shown in Figure 4.1. SmartIcons lets you select Lotus 1-2-3 commands and tasks quickly. (Remember: if you want to access SmartIcons, the Icons add-in and the Wysiwyg add-in must be running. If you don't see the SmartIcons at the right of your work area, see Lesson 10, "Working with Lotus 1-2-3's Add-Ins.")

Something's Missing If you have an EGA monitor, you will see only 12 of the 16 icons shown in Figure 4.1. You can still gain access to these four additional icons, and other icons not currently visible. Read the section in this lesson titled "Customizing Your Palette."

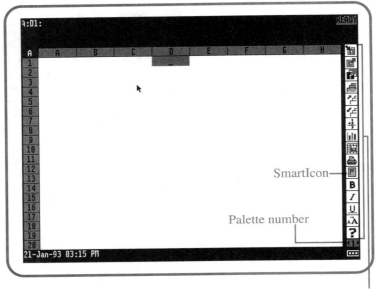

Figure 4.1 1-2-3's SmartIcons.

Getting to Know Lotus 1-2-3's SmartIcons

For convenience, SmartIcons are organized in *palettes*. In Version 3.4 you can switch among eight different palettes of powerful SmartIcons by clicking on the arrowheads on either side of the palette number. The palette number is displayed at the bottom of each palette column.

To see a description of any icon, just click and hold on the icon with the right mouse button. The description appears in the third line of 1-2-3's control panel. Table 4.1 gives you the functions of the SmartIcons presented on the start-up palette.

Custom Palette The start-up palette is also the *custom palette*—you can add the icons you use most often, or delete the ones you no longer use. The other seven palettes cannot be modified.

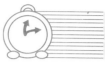

Table 4.1 The start-up SmartIcon palette.

Icon	Enables you to
	Save your worksheet to a disk.
	Retrieve a worksheet file.
	Read a file into memory after the current file.
	See three worksheets, stacked up.
	Move to the worksheet after this one.
	Move to the worksheet before this one.
	Calculate the sum of values in a range.
	Create, edit, or display a graph.
	Add your graph to the worksheet.
	Print a selected range of cells.
	Print the previous (or a specified) range.
	Add boldface to (or remove it from) a range.
	Add italics to (or clear them from) a range.

continues

23

Table 4.1 Continued.

Icon	Enables you to
U	Add single underlining to (or remove it from) data in a range.
ₐ$\vec{A}$	Cycle through available fonts for a range.
?	Start the Help system.

More About SmartIcons See the appendix at the end of the book for a list of the commonly used Lotus 1-2-3 SmartIcons.

Selecting SmartIcons

To select an icon from a SmartIcon palette with the keyboard:

1. Press Ctrl+F10.

2. Press ← or → to select a SmartIcon palette.

3. Press ↑ or ↓ to select a SmartIcon.

4. Press Enter to use the icon.

Mousing! It's easy to use the mouse to select an icon to perform a task—you just click on it! Click on the arrows surrounding the SmartIcon palette number to move through the palettes.

Customizing Your Palette

When you start 1-2-3 in WYSIWYG mode, palette 1 (the custom palette) appears with its set of specific SmartIcons. You can exchange icons on this palette with icons from other palettes. For example, here's how to replace SmartIcon 15 on palette 1 with an icon from the second palette:

1. Select icon palette 7.

2. Select the Add Icon SmartIcon. It looks like a stack of icons with a plus (+) sign.

3. Select the icon from palette 2 that you want to add to the custom palette.

   1-2-3 will replace the fifteenth icon on the custom palette, and return you to READY mode.

Gone? Not! When you replace a SmartIcon, you aren't physically moving it. Instead, the SmartIcon you've chosen is copied from its home palette to the custom palette. If the palette is full, 1-2-3 replaces the bottom icon.

You can remove icons from the custom palette. Here's how:

1. Select the icon palette 7.

2. Select the Del Icon SmartIcon. The start-up (custom) icon palette appears.

3. Click on the icon you want to remove (or highlight it with the arrow keys, and then press Enter). It is deleted.

Lesson 5

Inputting Data

In this lesson, you will learn how to input labels and values into a worksheet.

Plan Before You Begin

There are many types of data that you can enter into a 1-2-3 worksheet, and many ways to use this data to create a worksheet. Some spreadsheets are far more effective than others, so it pays to plan before you start typing.

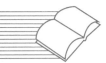

Data Types   You can enter dates, times, formulas, numbers, and text into 1-2-3 spreadsheets.

Suppose for a moment that you have a small stationery-store business. You want to keep track of the fourth-quarter sales revenues by individual items sold. Later you will analyze and graph these figures.

On paper, you see that the months of October, November, and December will occupy your columns. You also see that names of each item can occupy separate rows. Figure 5.1 shows the sample 1-2-3 spreadsheet.

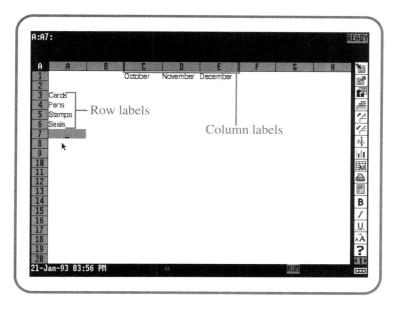

Figure 5.1 The sample stationery-store spreadsheet with labels.

Inputting Labels

It's easiest to begin a spreadsheet by typing in the labels. If you're following this business example, you could enter the column labels first, and then the row labels.

Labels Are   In a spreadsheet program, a *label* is any text you type into a cell. Labels are distin- 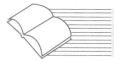 guished from values (numeric entries), formulas (equations that perform operations on values), and functions (a shorthand for complex formulas).

27

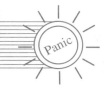

Can't Enter Data   You cannot enter data when the Main menu is displayed. Press Esc to return to the READY mode.

Column Labels

Column labels are arranged across your spreadsheet; to enter each one, type it and then press →. In the store example, you would follow these steps:

1. From cell A1, move to cell C1 by pressing → twice.

2. Type October in cell C1; press → when finished.

3. Type November in cell D1; press → when finished.

4. Type December in cell E1; press → when finished.

The Enter Key   When entering your data, you can always use the Enter key after each entry (instead of the directional arrow) if you want the entry accepted immediately. If you use this key, however, the cell pointer does not move to the next cell.

Row Labels

In this sample worksheet, the row labels extend down column A. Typing in row labels works much like typing in the column labels, except you'll use the down arrow between cell entries. Type the row label and press the down arrow after each entry. For the store example, follow these steps:

1. From cell A1, move to cell A3 by pressing ↓ twice.

2. Type `Cards` in A3 and press ↓.

3. Type `Pens` in A4 and press ↓.

4. Type `Stamps` in A5 and press ↓.

5. Type `Seals` in A6 and press ↓.

Wide Labels If your labels are too wide to fit into a cell, see Lesson 13 for instructions on changing column widths.

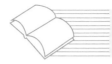

Inputting Values

The same approach used for entering labels will work for entering values: type the value, then move to another cell by using an arrow key (the value is then accepted). In the store example, you would follow these steps:

1. Position the cell pointer in cell C3.

2. Type 12 in C3 and press →.

3. Type 10 in D3 and press →.

4. Type 15 in E3 and press ↓.

5. Press ← twice to move the cell pointer back to cell C4.

6. Type 10 in C4 and press →.

7. Type 12 in D4 and press →.

8. Type 15 in E4 and press ↓.

9. Press ← twice to move the cell pointer back to cell C5.

Continue with these same steps to complete the data entry. If you're following the store example, your spreadsheet now looks like Figure 5.2.

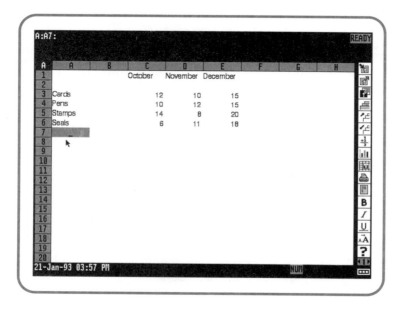

Figure 5.2   The completed sample worksheet.

In this lesson, you learned how to enter labels and values to build a simple spreadsheet. In the next lesson, you will learn how to use ranges for selecting, copying, naming, and deleting columns, rows and blocks of numbers. You will also learn how to use the pointer-movement keys.

Lesson 6
Using Ranges

In this lesson, you will learn how to select, copy, name, and delete cell ranges.

Range Basics

Sometimes, in the creation or modification of spreadsheets, you will need to work with selected groups of cells (ranges), rather than one individual cell or a whole worksheet. You can do a multitude of things easily to ranges—copy, format, delete, total, and move them—whether they are made up of columns, rows, or blocks of labels or numbers.

No Buffalo Here!   A *range* is any highlighted area of cells. It can be as small as two cells, or as large as the entire worksheet. For instance, you may need to format certain rows or columns of numbers to display dollars and cents.

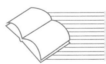

Selecting or Highlighting Ranges

Before you copy, move, or name a range of cells, you have to select the range. Only then will 1-2-3 know what you're going to do with the range.

Basically, you can select a range by typing in beginning and ending cell addresses, or by highlighting the range with the cell pointer or directional arrow. You can highlight the range by clicking and dragging the mouse. You can also enter a range name that you've previously assigned.

Selecting with Cell Addresses

The Copy command is a good way to learn how to type in a cell address at 1-2-3's prompt. To type a cell address, follow these steps:

1. Put the cell pointer in the cell you want to begin the range you're copying.

2. Press / (slash); the Main menu appears.

3. Select Copy from the Main menu. 1-2-3 asks which cell to copy from; FROM? appears in the control panel (see Figure 6.1).

4. Type the cell address from which the range is to start. For instance, if the range starts in C3, type in C3.

5. Enter two periods with no spaces (. .).

6. Type the cell address at which the range is to end. (If you're following the stationery-shop example, it ends in C6; the whole range will look like C3..C6.)

7. Press Enter.

You will be asked to give another range, showing just where you want to copy TO, but we're only practicing at this point. Stop the copy procedure by pressing Esc. Keep pressing Esc until the READY mode appears.

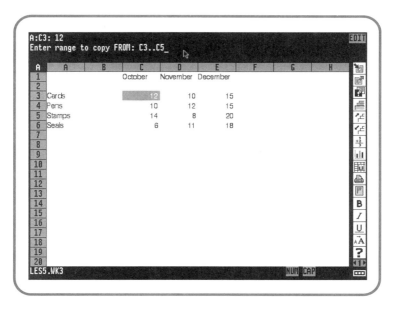

Figure 6.1 The Copy FROM? prompt is displayed in the control panel.

Selecting by Pointing

Here's how to use the keyboard to point to a range and select it:

33

1. Move the cell pointer onto the cell where the range begins.

2. Press / (slash) to call up the Main menu.

3. Select Copy from the Main menu.

4. When you see the Copy FROM? prompt, press ↓ until you've highlighted all the cells to be copied.

5. Press Enter.

To use your mouse to point and select, follow these steps:

1. Move the cell pointer onto the cell where the range begins.

2. Press / (slash) to call up the Main menu.

3. Click on Copy from the Main menu.

4. When you see the Copy FROM? prompt, point to the starting cell to be copied.

5. Press and hold the left mouse button. Drag the mouse until all the cells you want to select are highlighted.

6. When the range is highlighted, release the mouse button.

Release Me! Don't worry. You can deselect ranges easily by pressing Esc. Or you can move the mouse pointer away from the selected range and click.

Erasing a Range

To delete or erase a range, follow these steps:

1. Press / (slash) to call up the Main menu.

2. Choose Range from the Main menu.

3. Select Erase from the Range menu.

4. Enter the range name, then type an ending cell address (or point, click, hold, and drag to highlight the cell range).

5. Press Enter.

Naming Ranges of Cells

You can save time by *naming* a range of cells you use often, and then calling up the range name to move data into strategic places. Here's how to name a range:

1. Press / (slash) to call up the Main menu.

2. Select Range from the Main menu.

3. Select Name.

4. Select Create.

5. When 1-2-3 prompts you to Enter name:, type in a range name and press Enter. (In the sample worksheet, you could name the range holding the sales items, as items.)

6. Type in or point to the addresses that make up the range you are naming (for this example, choose cells A3..A6).

7. Press Enter and 1-2-3 will assign the range name to the cell range you've indicated.

Using Named Ranges in a Worksheet

To use the range name when specifying a range, follow these steps:

1. Press / (slash) to call up the Main menu.

2. Select Copy.

3. Type the range name you assigned (for our example, type items).

4. Press Enter. 1-2-3 will accept the new range, and ask where you want the copy to go.

5. Answer the TO? prompt, then press Enter.

6. If you are finished copying, press Esc until the READY mode appears.

Displaying a List of Range Names

Sometimes it's faster to choose a range name from a list. To get 1-2-3 to display a list of range names, follow these steps:

1. When prompted for a range (for example, in the Copy procedure), press F3. A list of range names appears.

2. Use ← or → to highlight the range name on the list.

3. Press Enter to select the range name.

Deleting a Range Name

To delete a range name, follow these steps:

1. Press / (slash) to call up the Main menu.

2. Choose Range from the Main menu.

3. Select Name.

4. Select Delete. A list of range names appears.

5. Highlight the name you want to delete from the list.

6. Press Enter. 1-2-3 deletes the range name, and returns to READY mode.

In this lesson, you learned how to use the Range command to select and copy ranges of data. You also learned how to name and erase range names. In the next lesson, you will discover how to save your worksheet.

Saving Your Data on a Worksheet

In this lesson, you will learn how to save your data on a worksheet in Lotus 1-2-3.

Save What?

When using any software, it's best to learn—*quickly*—how to save your work. If you don't save your work, all your efforts disappear when you clear the workspace, get a new file, or exit the program.

Saving is a simple process in Lotus 1-2-3. The basic command is /File Save, which copies your worksheet to your fixed drive or diskette. Then it's permanently yours.

Some Rules

When saving, you're going to be asked to give your worksheet a name, and "Hey you!" won't work.

1. Your file name can have up to eight characters. (Remember: 1-2-3 adds an extension of .WK3 automatically.)

2. Your file name can be composed of letters, numbers, and the underscore (_) or hyphen (-) characters, or a combination of these.

3. Don't use any blank spaces. You may never see your worksheet again if you do!

4. Don't use these characters: / \ = + ; : | ! ? * < > "

Just stick with the facts, as the guy from Dragnet says; in 1-2-3, stick with eight characters, numbers, the underscore, and hyphen. You'll save yourself from a great big headache!

Saving a Lotus 1-2-3 Worksheet

After you make sure that 1-2-3 is in READY mode, follow these steps to save a newly created worksheet:

1. Press / (slash) to call up the Main menu.

2. Select File from the Main menu.

3. Select Save. The control panel displays the path and a filename for new worksheets (example: File0001.WK3).

4. Press Esc. Get ready to enter your file's name on the *filename line*. Line 3 of the control panel shows a horizontal list of the files saved in 1-2-3 (see Figure 7.1).

5. Press Esc again; the *edit cursor* (a flashing pointer) will take its place at the end of your data directory's name.

39

6. Type in your filename:

If the directory showing is the one you want to use to store your file, accept it and type in your file name.

If you want to use a different directory, use the Back-space key to wipe out the name of the default directory, type in the one you want to use, and then enter your filename.

7. Press Enter; 1-2-3 will save your worksheet.

 Quick Save Use the Save SmartIcon from any palette to save a worksheet quickly (either new or modified).

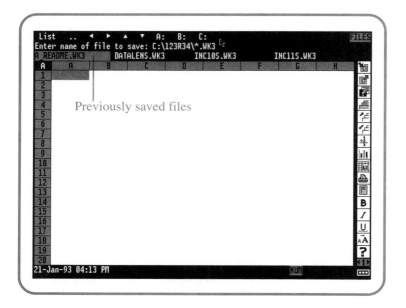

Figure 7.1 List of files saved in 1-2-3.

Saving and Replacing

You can change a file saved previously in one of two ways:

- Give the worksheet a new name (this way you have copies of both the old and new versions). The steps for saving a worksheet with a new name are the same as those for saving a whole new worksheet.

- Do a *save and replace*, which updates the version of the same worksheet with the same filename. It's up to you!

To save and replace a 1-2-3 worksheet so it keeps its original filename, follow these steps:

1. Press / (slash) to call up the Main menu.

2. Choose File from the Main menu.

3. Select Save. You'll be shown the existing file name in the control panel.

4. Press Enter; 1-2-3 will prompt you to Cancel, Replace or BackUp.

5. Highlight one of these options:

   Cancel will leave the existing file just as it is, and return you to READY mode.

   Replace will overwrite the existing file on your disk while saving the modified version.

   BackUp will save the old version of the file under a .BAK extension.

6. Once you've chosen an option, press Enter to save your worksheet.

41

Retrieving a Lotus 1-2-3 Worksheet

In this lesson, you will learn how to retrieve a worksheet saved previously.

Getting It Back

The longer you work with 1-2-3, the more of a "history" of documents you build up. Fortunately, 1-2-3 makes it easy to bring back (or *retrieve*) worksheets you've created and saved in the past.

Save First   Before you retrieve a different file, *be sure to save any current work.* The retrieval process erases what you have on-screen, automatically.

Here are the steps you'll take to bring back an existing worksheet:

1. Display the Main menu by pressing / (slash).

2. Choose File from the Main menu.

3. Select Retrieve. Names of worksheet files saved in the current directory appear across the third line of the control panel. 1-2-3 lists the files alphabetically, as shown in Figure 8.1.

List indicator

Figure 8.1 Saved worksheet files.

4. Use the arrow keys to scroll through the filenames, and highlight (or click on it with the mouse) the filename of the worksheet you are retrieving. (If you know the filename, press Esc; enter the name of the file you want to retrieve, and the prompt will appear. You can then type in the filename or click on it with the mouse.)

5. Press Enter. The retrieval is complete.

Full-Screen File List

If scrolling through the control panel's list of files seems too slow, you may find it's quicker to display a full-screen listing.

 The fastest way to bring up this list is by clicking on the Retrieve SmartIcon found on palette 1.

Another way to bring up the full-screen file list is to press F3, or click the mouse on the List indicator in the top left corner of your screen (see Figure 8.1).

In both cases, your spreadsheet will disappear—and a list of files in the current directory will fill the screen, as shown in Figure 8.2.

To select the file you want to retrieve from the list:

* Click on its filename.

* Use the arrow keys to move to the filename you want. Once it's highlighted, press Enter.

Disaster Relief

We all make mistakes, and 1-2-3's authors were kind enough to build in a "back door," in case you forget to save your work before starting the Retrieve process.

In fact, if you haven't made any changes to the retrieved file, you can return to your previous worksheet—and save it. If you find yourself in this situation, take these steps:

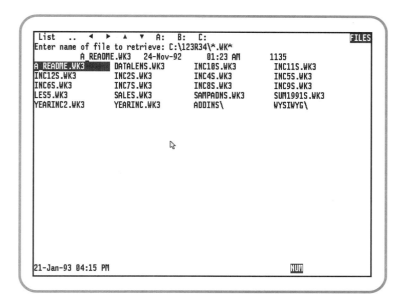

```
List  ..  ◀  ▶  ▲  ▼  A:  B:  C:                        FILES
Enter name of file to retrieve: C:\123R34\*.WK*
          A_README.WK3   24-Nov-92      01:23 AM    1135
A_README.WK3      DATALENS.WK3    INC10S.WK3      INC11S.WK3
INC12S.WK3        INC2S.WK3       INC4S.WK3       INC5S.WK3
INC6S.WK3         INC7S.WK3       INC8S.WK3       INC9S.WK3
LES5.WK3          SALES.WK3       SAMPADNS.WK3    SUM1991S.WK3
YEARINC2.WK3      YEARINC.WK3     ADDINS\         WYSIWYG\




                              ▷



21-Jan-93 04:15 PM                              NUM
```

Figure 8.2   Directory contents, as shown by the List feature.

1. Look at the status line of the work area; the UNDO indicator should appear there. If it does not, use the following tip. If it does, go on to step 2.

Next Time!   If the UNDO indicator isn't displayed on the status line, you won't be able to save the file that's been deleted, but you can protect yourself should this ever happen again. Turn on the Undo feature by selecting /Worksheet Global Default Other Undo Enable and Update.

2. Press Alt+F4 to undo the Retrieve. The previous worksheet will appear.

 You can Undo quickly by using the Undo SmartIcon found in palette 5.

In this lesson, you learned how to retrieve a worksheet file saved previously. In the next lesson, you will learn how to create formulas and use functions.

Lesson 9

Working with Formulas and Functions

In this lesson, you will learn how to build, enter, and edit formulas, and use functions in worksheets.

Spreadsheet Power

You can place a lot of letters and numbers into spreadsheet cells. You can enter numbers in various formats—including fractions, decimals, and dates. You can put in letters (as labels) that describe the content of particular rows or columns.

Here's something else you can put into your worksheet's cells, something that gives your 1-2-3 worksheet real oomph and power: formulas.

Calculatin' A *formula* performs calculations based on the numbers in other cells—but it will only get the right answer if you build it according to a specific order of operations (see "Order of Precedence," later in this lesson).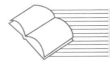

You can build your own worksheet-unique formulas— and many 1-2-3 users are very sophisticated at building

47

formulas. You can also use some built-in formulas called @*functions* (pronounced "at-functions").

Formulas are really what make your spreadsheet worth the time and effort. You can use them to:

- Add up a group of numbers.

- Find and display the average of a range of numbers.

- Analyze the values in groups of cells statistically.

- Perform a "what-if" analysis, using different numbers to explore different possibilities.

Building Your Own Formulas

Suppose you want to add values you have entered in cells C3 through C6, placing the total in cell C7. Follow these steps:

1. Retrieve your worksheet (see Lesson 8 for instructions).

2. Move the cell pointer to cell C7.

3. Press + on the number pad (all 1-2-3 formulas must begin with a number, or with one of these characters: + − @.

4. Type C3+C4+C5+C6.

5. Press Enter.

The result appears in cell C7. Look at the first line of the control panel (as shown in Figure 9.1) to see your formula.

Formula   Result of formula

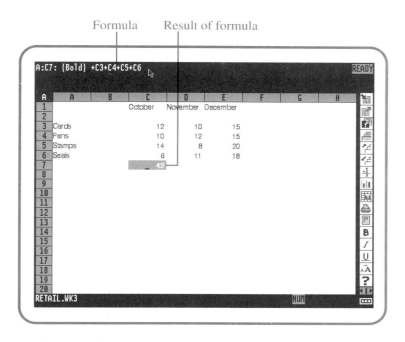

Figure 9.1   A formula is displayed in line 1 of the control panel.

Formula Operators

Most formulas are somewhat lengthy, and do all sorts of things—like add, subtract, multiply, divide, and more. Mathematical symbols—*operators*—tell 1-2-3 how to treat the values that appear in your formula. Table 9.1 shows the operators you can use.

To enter a series of values in cells A1, B1, and C1 and enter a formula in D1 determining the average of these values, you would enter the formula (A1+B1+C1)/3 in cell D1. This tells 1-2-3 to add the values in cells A1, B1, and C1 and divide the total by 3. The result is then inserted in cell D1.

49

Table 9.1   1-2-3's formula operators.

Operator	Description
+	Add
−	Subtract
*	Multiply
/	Divide
^	Treat as exponent
>	Is greater than
<	Is less than
>=	Is greater than or equal to
<=	Is less than or equal to
<>	Is not equal to

Order of Precedence

Spreadsheet programs perform operations in a formula in particular specific order; some operators (such as multiplication) have precedence over others (such as addition). The order in which the operators appear in the formula will affect its result. This *order of precedence* should be as follows:

- First: exponential equations

- Second: multiplication and division

- Third: addition and subtraction

Parentheses control the order of operations. For example, in the averaging formula, if you leave out the parentheses, you'll get the wrong answer! The value in

C1 will be divided by 3, and that result will be added to A1+B1. To determine the total of A1 through C1 first, you need to enclose that group of values in parentheses.

Wrong Answer   If your formula doesn't work or you get an error, check for a closing parenthesis to accompany each opening parenthesis. Next, check the order of operations. A rule to remember: "*My Dear Aunt Sally!*" (multiply, divide, add, subtract).

Editing Formulas

If you must edit your formula, and prefer not to type it in again, follow these steps:

1. Move your cell pointer to the cell that displays the formula you intend to edit.

2. Press F2 (the Edit key). This puts 1-2-3 in EDIT mode.

3. Make your changes (use Backspace to delete characters you don't want).

4. Press Enter; after making your changes, 1-2-3 puts you back in READY mode.

Check Your Formulas   If you have a complicated worksheet with many formulas, sometimes you may need to display all of them. Choose Worksheet from the Main menu, followed by Select Global Format. Then choose Text. The formulas will appear in their appropriate on-screen locations. Return to normal display by selecting /Worksheet Global Format General.

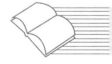

1-2-3's Functions

You'll find that 1-2-3 comes with a set of useful preset functions. (These must begin with an @ sign. A table of 1-2-3 functions is included in the back of this book.)

You can, for instance, total the column of values in cells C3 through C6 by typing @sum(C3..C6) in cell A11. To assign this function, follow these steps:

1. Using the arrow keys, place the cell pointer in cell A11.

2. Type @SUM(.

3. Enter the range of cells to total by typing in the addresses, pointing to the range, or using a range name.

4. Type the closing parenthesis,). The result in our example should read @SUM(C3..C6).

5. Press Enter. The result will be placed in cell A11.

Sum It Up To total a range quickly, select the Sum SmartIcon from palette 1.

In this lesson, you learned how to create and edit formulas. You also learned that 1-2-3 has a set of built-in formulas that are easy to use. In the next lesson, you will learn how to use three add-in programs that give you the capability to check formulas, change them, and analyze data in a worksheet file to solve what-if problems.

Lesson 10

Working with Lotus 1-2-3's Add-Ins

In this lesson, you will learn how to use the three special add-in programs—Auditor, Backsolver, and Solver.

Attaching an Add-In

Before using an add-in program, you must load it into memory. From your worksheet screen, follow these steps:

1. Press Alt+F10. A menu appears.

2. Choose Load, and then select the add-in. (For our example, select Auditor.)

3. Choose a key combination that will activate the add-in. (For our example, pick Alt+F7.) Then move the cursor to 1, and select it by clicking or pressing the Enter key.

4. Press Esc to return to your worksheet.

Once the add-in has been attached, you can invoke it at any time during the 1-2-3 session by pressing the function key to which it is attached (in this example, Alt+F7).

Auditor

If you have an enormous worksheet containing many formulas, it can be time-consuming to analyze the structure of the worksheet, locate formulas, and find the sources of errors. 1-2-3 provides an add-in program, Auditor, that can help you:

- Track formulas and their relationships.

- Locate possible circular references.

- Assure that certain formulas are calculating in the correct order of precedence.

When you activate Auditor (using its key combination), a menu appears, as shown in Figure 10.1. These settings display the current Audit range and Audit mode. The default Audit range includes all worksheets in all files in memory, and the default Audit mode is Highlight.

Table 10.1 shows Auditor's commands and the tasks they perform when you activate them.

Table 10.1 Auditor's commands.

Command	Task
Circs	Shows the cells making up a circular reference.
Dependents	Shows which formulas in the audit range refer to one specific cell.
Formulas	Shows which formulas make up the audit range.
Options	Lets you change audit range and audit mode.

Command	Task
Precedents	Shows which cells in the audit range are data sources for a specific formula.
Quit	Returns you to 1-2-3's READY mode.
Recalc-List	Shows all recalculated formulas, in order.

Figure 10.1   Auditor's Main menu.

Circs

To give you an idea of how to use Auditor, let's look at the Circs option.

A *circular reference* occurs when a formula refers (directly or indirectly) to itself. For instance, if cell A7 contains the formula @AVG(A7..A15), the circular reference is *direct* (A7 is in the formula). If cell A1 contains +A2, cell A2 contains +A3, and cell A3 contains +A1, the circular reference is *indirect* (you loop back to the starting point, cell A1). Either a direct or indirect circular reference will make 1-2-3 display the CIRC indicator near the bottom of your screen (as in Figure 10.2).

Simply seeing the CIRC indicator doesn't help you determine *where* that circular reference might be. That's why you need the Auditor program itself. Here's an example of how to use Auditor to identify the circular reference:

1. Invoke Auditor (Alt+F7 or whatever key combination you defined).

2. Select Circs from the Auditor menu. Auditor displays the cells involved in a circular reference.

3. Press Esc three times to return to your worksheet and the READY mode.

Detaching an Add-In

The more add-ins you attach, the more memory 1-2-3 requires. Therefore, you should detach any add-ins you are not using. To detach Auditor—or any add-in—follow these steps:

1. Press Alt+F10.

2. Choose Remove from the menu, and press Enter.

3. Select Auditor (or the appropriate add-in).

4. Press Esc.

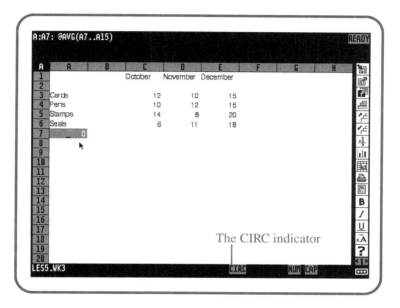

Figure 10.2   A circular reference in a 1-2-3 worksheet.

Backsolver

Perhaps you have a specific target to achieve for the retail sales profit margin, and you want to see what total sales must be reached to attain that target. Backsolver is an add-in that lets you calculate a formula to achieve a value (your target profit margin, for example) by changing one or more variables that affect the results of the formula.

It's like playing Jeopardy. You provide the answer, and Backsolver provides the question (the variables). If you change one of the variables, Backsolver will tell you how the change affects the other variables, assuming the answer remains the same.

Caution: Save Those Original Values When you use Backsolver, 1-2-3 replaces the original values in the variable cells with its own answers. If you don't want to lose your original values, either save your file before using Backsolver, or make a copy of the original values in another location.

First, you must attach the Backsolver add-in. (You learned to do this earlier in this lesson.) Next, with the appropriate worksheet open, follow these steps:

1. In a cell (which becomes the *formula cell*) or range, type in the formula you want Backsolver to use.

2. Decide on the result you want to reach, and the variables you will change to reach it.

3. Press Alt+F10, select Load, then select Backsolver.

4. When the Backsolver menu appears, choose Formula-Cell.

5. Indicate the name of the range (or the address of the formula cell) in which you typed your formula in step 1.

6. Choose Value.

7. Type in the value you want the formula cell's formula to give you. You can enter a formula instead; Backsolver will convert it to a number before solving the problem.

8. Choose Adjustable.

9. Identify (either by address or range name) the cells containing values you will let Backsolver change.

10. Choose Solve.

11. When Backsolver finishes, choose Quit; READY mode reappears.

Solver

Solver lets you explore different results of your formula by running different combinations of values through it—a process called *what-if analysis*. If you want to improve the profitability of your business, for instance, use Solver to experiment with different combinations of sales quotas and cost cuts.

Before using this add-in, first enter *logical formulas* into your worksheet; these tell Solver the conditions you want it to meet while calculating your answer. If you want an interest rate below 13 percent, for example, you can specify it with a logical formula such as +LOAN<.13.

Solver then uses the cells you specify (as well as other information in the worksheet) to help you analyze and solve problems. Using Solver is complicated, beyond the scope of this book, but you can find help for it in Lesson 17.

This lesson previewed three of 1-2-3's powerful add-ins, Auditor, Backsolver, and Solver. The next lesson moves into copying and moving cells, with special emphasis on absolute and relative cell references.

Lesson 11

Copying and Moving Cells in Lotus 1-2-3

In this lesson, you'll learn to move and copy the contents of your 1-2-3 worksheet cells.

You may have a great formula you'd like to use elsewhere in your worksheet. 1-2-3 makes copying and moving the contents of cells a simple task.

In this lesson you'll begin with the basics of copying and moving, and then move into the more sophisticated topic of using relative and absolute cell references. You'll need to know about cell referencing if you're going to move or copy formulas.

Copying Cell Contents

You can copy the contents of one cell, or the contents of many cells (a range of cells). For instance, you may need to copy a range of numbers located in cells C7 through C12 to the location B7 through B12. Here are the steps to take:

1. Select Copy from the Main menu. The copy FROM: prompt appears (see Figure 11.1).

2. Perform one of the following:

- If you're copying a single cell, move the cell pointer to that cell or type its address.

- If you're copying a range of cells, select the range of cells to copy, by typing the range or by pointing to it.

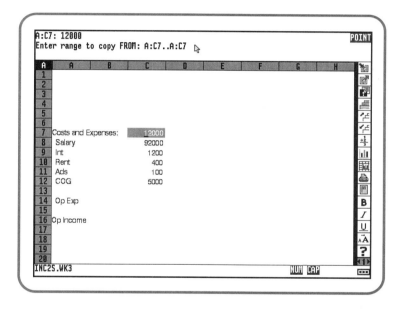

Figure 11.1   The copy FROM: prompt appears as the Copy command is selected.

3. Press Enter. The copy TO: prompt appears.

4. Perform one of the following:

- If you are copying one cell to another cell, move the pointer to the destination cell or type its address.

61

- If you are copying a range of cells to an area of identical size, put the cell pointer on the cell that begins the destination range, or type that cell's address.

- If the destination range has a size or shape different from that of the range being copied, either highlight the destination range or type its address.

5. Press Enter. 1-2-3 copies the indicated range of cells, as shown in Figure 11.2.

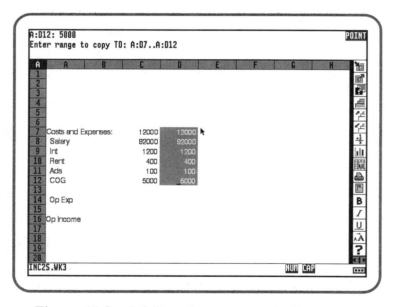

Figure 11.2   1-2-3 copies a range of cells.

If you want to copy a range of cells quickly, first select it, then select the Copy SmartIcon from palette 5, and then choose the destination range.

Moving Cells

Moving cells works almost exactly like copying cells. The difference? You're physically moving the cell's actual contents, rather than a duplicate of those contents, to another location. Follow these steps to move cells:

1. Choose Move from the Main menu. The move FROM: prompt appears.

2. Perform one of the following:

   • If you're moving a single cell, move the cell pointer to that cell, or type its address.

   • If you're moving a range of cells, select the range of cells to move (type the range or point to it). For example, to move the cell range indicated in the earlier section, type in A5..A25.

3. Press Enter. The move TO: prompt appears.

4. Perform one of the following:

   • If you are moving one cell to another cell, move the pointer to the destination cell or type its address.

   • If you are moving a range of cells to an identically-sized area, position the cell pointer at the beginning cell of the destination range, or type the cell's address. (For our example, you would type B5..B25.)

   • If the destination range differs in size or shape from the range being moved, either type the destination range or highlight it.

5. Press Enter. 1-2-3 removes the cells from their original position, and places them in the new location.

You can move a selected range of cells quickly with the Move SmartIcon on palette 5. Before you select the icon, be sure to select the range you want to move.

Relative and Absolute References

1-2-3 doesn't just blindly move and copy; it tries to anticipate your needs. For example, let's say you have a formula that adds the contents of a column. When you copy that formula into a different column, you want the formula to report the total for the new column, not the old one.

1-2-3 knows that you probably want to copy the meaning of the formula, not the actual cell references. That's why all cell references in 1-2-3 are *relative* unless you specify otherwise. The formulas work "relative to" their surroundings—when you move or copy a formula, its cell addresses change to reflect its new place in the worksheet.

For instance, you could place a formula in cell A5 to average three numbers in column A, (A1..A3). If you copied this formula to B5, 1-2-3 would change your formula automatically to reflect the new cell addresses. The formula +(A1+A2+A3)/3 would become +(B1+B2+B3)/3 when copied to B5.

There are times, however, when you may need to override this relative referencing, to make a cell address *absolute*. For example, you may want the formula in cell A5 to remain +(+A1+A2+A3)/3 no matter where you put a copy of it.

64

To create an absolute address to a cell, you must enter a dollar sign ($) before both the column and row of each cell address in the formula. For our example in cell A5, it would look like this: +($A$1+$A$2+$A$3)/3. See Figure 11.3.

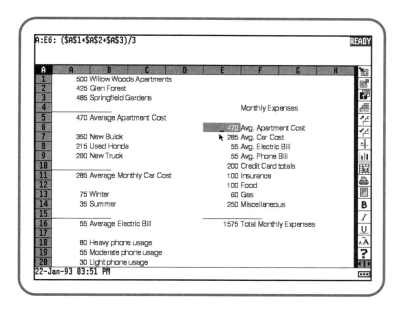

Figure 11.3   A formula indicating absolute cell reference.

Referencing   You can create a mix of absolute and relative cell referencing. For instance, you can use $A10 to indicate an absolute reference for column A, with a relative address for row 10.

This lesson showed you how to copy and move cell contents throughout your worksheet. You also learned how to change the relative cell reference to absolute. Read Lesson 12 to learn how to edit and delete contents of cells.

Lesson 12
Editing, Deleting, and Recalculating Cells

In this lesson, you'll learn how to edit and delete cell contents, and recalculate formulas manually.

No one's perfect! Sometimes we need to delete a little here, and add a little there. 1-2-3 enables you to make such changes—and more—with a minimum of effort.

Cell Editing

To edit a cell, just highlight it and press F2, then use the editing keys shown in Table 12.1 to make your changes. Here are the exact steps to follow:

1. Move the cell pointer to the cell to be edited.

2. Press F2. The EDIT indicator appears (see Figure 12.1).

3. Make your changes, using the keys shown in Table 12.1.

4. Press Enter to record changes and return to the READY mode.

Edit mode indicator

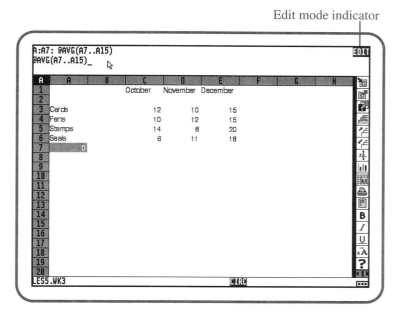

Figure 12.1   The Edit mode is activated.

Table 12.1   Major editing keys.

Key	Performs
Arrows	← or → moves one character left or right in the edit line.
Backspace	Moves the cursor left, deleting a character.
Del	Deletes the character the cursor highlights.
End	Cursor moves rightward to the end of the edit line.
Esc	Removes the characters in the edit line.
Home	Cursor moves leftward to the start of the edit line.
Ins	Toggles between INSERT and OVERTYPE mode.

67

Don't Mess Up   Be judicious when making your cell changes. Watch for reversed parentheses, extra quote marks, and forgotten dollar signs (which indicate absolute cell references).

Deleting Cell Contents

When you delete the contents of a cell, the cell is still there; it's just emptied. Follow these steps to erase the contents of a single cell:

1. Move the cell pointer to the cell you've chosen to erase.

2. Select Range from the Main menu.

3. Choose Erase.

4. Press Enter. The cell is erased, and replaced with a blank cell.

Instructions for erasing a range of cells are given in Lesson 6. To delete entire rows or columns, see Lesson 14.

Quick Delete   Use the Delete SmartIcon to erase cells and ranges of cells. Highlight the range to be erased and then select this SmartIcon from palette 5.

Recalculating Formulas

1-2-3 calculates formulas automatically when you enter them into your worksheet. Every time you enter numbers into cells that are referenced in the formula, 1-2-3

68

recalculates again. If you have a large spreadsheet, waiting for the formulas to recalculate can be annoying.

One solution is to set 1-2-3 for manual recalculation, so you can recalculate whenever you like. The following procedure sets 1-2-3 so that it recalculates whenever you press the F9 key.

1. From the Worksheet menu, choose Global.

2. Choose Recalc.

3. Select Manual (see Figure 12.2).

Upon returning to your worksheet, you will have set 1-2-3 to calculate (or recalculate) only when you press F9 (the Calc key). You can change back to automatic recalculation by following steps 1 and 2 again, this time choosing Automatic instead of Manual.

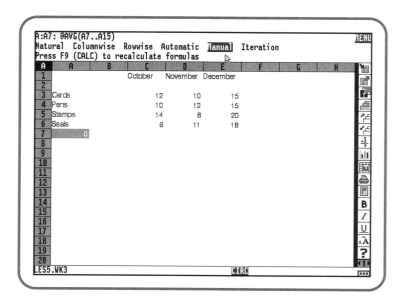

Figure 12.2   Selecting Manual recalculation.

Don't Forget! If you set your spreadsheet for Manual recalculation, you must press F9 to perform the actual calculations. It's critical that you remember to press F9 before quitting and saving the worksheet.

Works the Same The Calc Smart-Icon, from icon palette 3, acts just like the F9 (Calc) key in recalculating formulas.

This lesson showed you how to use 1-2-3's powerful editing capabilities. Next, you'll learn how to format your worksheet.

Lesson 13

Changing the
Look of a
Worksheet

In this lesson, you will learn how to change the cell format and column widths, and how to align labels.

1-2-3 offers you many options for customizing the appearance of your worksheet. You can use these options to make your worksheets look especially distinctive for others to enjoy by following the directions in this lesson, and continuing on in Lesson 14.

Changing Cell Format

You have the choice of several different cell formats, ways of displaying values and labels in worksheet cells. For instance, you can display some values with one decimal place (25.5) and others with a percent sign (25%).

Change the cell format in a range with /Range Format. To change cells to display currency, for instance, follow these steps.

1. Move the cell pointer to a cell, or select a range of cells.

2. Press / (slash) to call up the Main menu.

3. Select Range from the Main menu.

71

4. For this example, select Format, then Currency.

5. Press Enter. This accepts the default number of 2 decimal places.

6. Press Enter again to complete the format for currency.

Table 13.1 lists the major numeric format options, and their effects on the way values are displayed.

Table 13.1   Major numeric formats.

Format	Affects the Displayed Values This Way
,(comma)	Commas separate thousands; 15 or fewer decimal places; minus sign or parentheses to show negative numbers; and a leading zero for decimal places. Example: 987344 can become 987,344.
Currency	Commas separate thousands; 15 or fewer decimal places; minus sign or parentheses indicate negative numbers; currency symbols included. Example: 2345.0 can become $2,345.00.
Fixed	15 or fewer decimal places; minus sign indicates negative numbers; decimal values have a leading zero. Example: 23.89 can become 24.
General	Minus sign indicates negative numbers; no commas separate thousands; no trailing zeros. Example: 134,00.20 becomes 13400.2.
Percent	Percentages with 15 or fewer decimal places. Example: .089 becomes 8.9%.
Scientific	Shows values in scientific notation; 15 or fewer decimal places; exponent from −99 through +99. Example: −22 becomes −2.20E+01.
Text	Formulas shown as entered (not as calculated values). Example: 25 could be displayed as A12/A3, or any other formula.

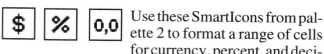

| $ | % | 0,0 |

Use these SmartIcons from palette 2 to format a range of cells for currency, percent, and decimal places.

Changing Column Widths

1-2-3 sets all column widths to 9 characters, by default. Often this width isn't sufficient to display numbers that you've formatted as currency with 2 decimal places, so you will see asterisks instead, as in Figure 13.1.

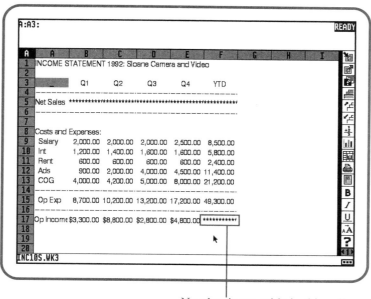

Number is too wide in this cell

Figure 13.1 Asterisks replace a lengthy number until columns are reformatted to hold the wide number.

To widen all the columns in a worksheet, follow these instructions:

1. Press / (slash) to call up the Main menu.

2. Select Worksheet.

3. Choose Global (which affects the entire worksheet).

4. Select Col-Width, as shown in Figure 13.2.

5. Type in a new column width (from 1 to 240) and press Enter.

Single Column Width, Quick Change   You can also change the width of a single column. Put the cursor in the column you want to change, and use the /Worksheet Column Set-width series of commands.

Use Arrow   If you don't know the exact width you want a column to have when it expands, use → and ← to test different widths visually before you choose a column width number. Each time you press →, the column grows wider.

Aligning Labels

Column labels typically don't line up with the figures in the columns until they are realigned by inserting a *label prefix*. By default, labels are left-aligned; columns of values are right-aligned.

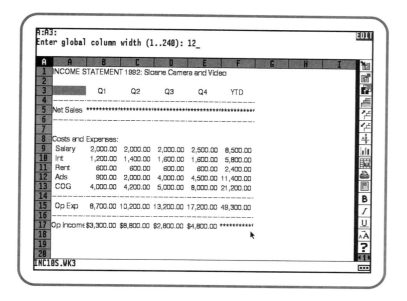

Figure 13.2 Selecting Col-Width to widen a column.

Table 13.2 shows 1-2-3's label prefixes, and how they affect label alignment.

Table 13.2 1-2-3 Label Prefixes.

Prefix	Cell Display	Alignment
'	label	left
^	label	centered
"	label	right
\	labellabellabel	repeating

To change the default of a left-aligned label, type in the alternative label prefix when entering the label (see Figure 13.3). You can also change the alignment of a label (or range of labels) by following these steps.

1. Press / (slash) to call up the Main menu.

2. Choose Range.

3. Choose Label.

4. Choose an alignment (Left, Right, or Center).

5. Type a cell or range of cells.

6. Press Enter.

   To change the formatting of a label quickly, use these SmartIcons from palette 2.

   To add emphasis in a worksheet, use these Smart-Icons from palette 1 to add bold, italic, and underline formatting attributes to labels.

Centered label

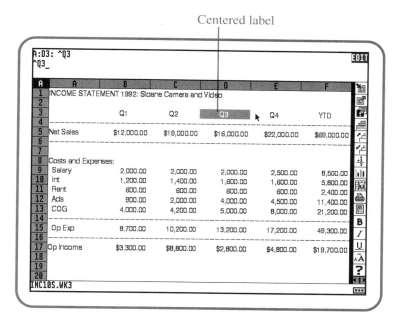

Figure 13.3 Label prefix for centered labels.

In this lesson, you learned how to customize your worksheet through changing the cell format, column widths, and aligning labels. In the next lesson, you will learn how to insert rows, delete unwanted rows, and use automatic formatting.

Lesson 14
More
Formatting

In this lesson, you will learn how to insert and delete rows and columns, and use automatic formatting techniques.

Inserting Rows and Columns

Special formatting techniques can help you really show off your worksheet. For instance, try inserting several blank rows and columns in your worksheet to set off the data. The added "white space" can give your worksheet an attractive look, as well as making it easier to read and understand.

In Figure 14.1, notice how extra space (inserted rows) was used to set off column labels. The space was then filled with asterisks.

To insert a row or column, begin by moving the cell pointer to any cell in the row below where you want the new row to appear, or the column to the right of where you want the new column to appear.

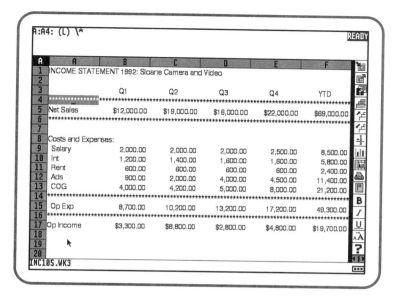

Figure 14.1   Using added space to set off data.

1. Press / (slash) to call up the Main menu.

2. Select Worksheet.

3. Select Insert.

4. Choose Row or Column.

5. When you are prompted, enter a range, press Enter.

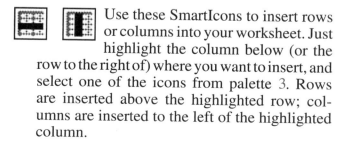

Use these SmartIcons to insert rows or columns into your worksheet. Just highlight the column below (or the row to the right of) where you want to insert, and select one of the icons from palette 3. Rows are inserted above the highlighted row; columns are inserted to the left of the highlighted column.

79

Delete To delete a row or column, follow the above steps and select Delete in step 3.

Automatic Formatting

How would you like to enter data and format the cell in the same step? With the Automatic Formatting option, 1-2-3 formats cells according to the way values look when you enter them. If you enter $35.00, for instance, 1-2-3 formats the cell as Currency, 2 decimal places. Here is how to turn this feature on:

1. Press / (slash) to call up the Main menu.

2. Select Worksheet.

3. Choose Global.

4. Select Format.

5. Select Other.

6. Select Automatic.

Any cells that haven't been formatted with the /Range Format command are now set for automatic formatting.

In this lesson, you learned how to insert and delete rows and columns, and to use automatic formatting techniques. In the next lesson, you will learn how to further enhance your worksheets by using Wysiwyg.

Lesson 15
Enhancing Your Spreadsheet with Wysiwyg

In this lesson, you will learn how to enhance your worksheet further using Wysiwyg.

What's Wysiwyg?

Wysiwyg is an add-in program that lets you give your spreadsheet a publishable look. The funny-sounding name (pronounced "wizzy-wig") stands for "what you see is what you get," and what it says is what it means—the feature shows you, on-screen, a close replica of your final printed worksheet.

Attach It First   If Wysiwyg isn't attached automatically when 1-2-3 loads, you will need to attach it. Directions for attachment are given in the first section of Lesson 10.

Changing Type (Font) Styles

Follow these steps to change the font for a range in the worksheet:

81

1. Activate the Wysiwyg menu by pressing : (colon).

2. Select Format, and then choose Font.

3. To choose your typeface and type size, select a font by choosing its number.

4. When the prompt appears, type the range you are changing; press Enter. Figure 15.1 shows the worksheet with its new font settings.

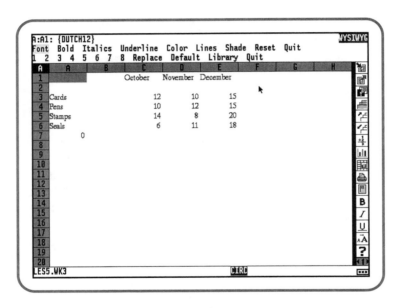

Figure 15.1 A worksheet with font settings created in Wysiwyg.

Change Default You don't have to keep the same default font; to change it, just select :Format Font Default Update, and when the Font Settings dialog box appears, select your new default font.

Adding Borders

You can lend special emphasis to particular areas of your spreadsheet if you add borders around them. Here's how:

1. Activate the Wysiwyg menu by pressing : (colon).

2. Choose Format.

3. Select Lines.

4. Select Outline.

5. Type in, at the prompt, the range you want to border; press Enter. The border will appear (see Figure 15.2).

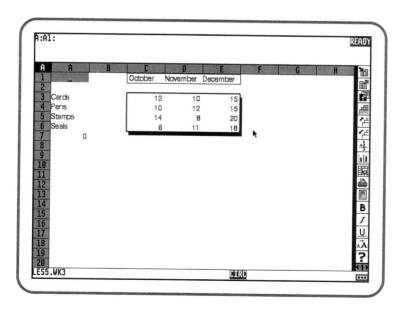

Figure 15.2   The worksheet with added borders.

 **Add Lines** To add lines around, underneath, to the left or right, or above single cells, use the :Format Lines command.

Selecting Frames

You can make changes in the frame that surrounds your worksheet (for example, showing a ruler) by following these steps:

1. Activate the Wysiwyg menu by pressing : (colon).

2. Choose Display from the Wysiwyg menu.

3. Select Options.

4. Select Frame.

5. Select Special from the options that appear.

6. Select Inches. The ruler line (the change in our example) appears at the top of the frame.

7. Select Quit two times. You are returned to READY mode.

Line Height

If you want to change the line height of your worksheet's rows, the procedure is simple. Use these steps:

1. Activate the Wysiwyg menu by pressing : (colon).

2. Choose Worksheet.

3. Select Row.

4. Select Set-Height.

5. Select the row (or range of rows) you want changed.

6. Press Enter.

7. Type in the new line height, in points.

8. Press Enter.

Turning the Grid On and Off

Using Wysiwyg, you can turn the grid lines on and off from your worksheet. To turn the grid lines on or off, follow these steps:

1. Activate the Wysiwyg menu by pressing : (colon).

2. Choose Display.

3. Select Options.

4. Select Grid.

5. Select Yes to turn on the grid lines and No to turn off the grid lines.

In this lesson, you learned how to use some of Wysiwyg's features. Of course this feature has numerous possibilities. Refer to your 1-2-3 Reference manual for more ideas. In the next lesson, you will learn how to print your worksheet.

Lesson 16
Printing Details

In this lesson, you will learn how to print a worksheet, print a screen, add headers and footers, print in land-scape, and learn how to print worksheet formulas.

What's New?

Version 3.4 of 1-2-3 offers the ability to print in landscape mode on your dot-matrix printer (explained in a later section of this lesson). 1-2-3 also includes many new and improved printer drivers, among them drivers for the Hewlett-Packard LaserJet III, IIID, IIIP, and the LaserJet IIISi. New drivers are also available for IBM's LaserPrinter 4019 and 4029 models.

Quick Printing

When your worksheet is ready to print, you can use 1-2-3's Print commands to print your worksheet. To print a speci-fied range of cells, follow these steps:

1. Press / (slash) to call up the Main menu.

2. Choose Print.

3. Choose Printer.

4. Choose Range.

5. Press Home, to move to A1 (the starting point of our example range).

6. Press . (period) to anchor the cell pointer in A1.

7. Move the cell pointer to the rightmost bottom cell on your spreadsheet.

8. Press Enter to accept the print range (in this example, A1..F16).

9. Press Align to ensure your printer will begin printing each page at the top of the paper.

10. Choose Go to begin printing.

11. Select Page to advance the paper to the top of the next page.

12. Select Quit to return to the Worksheet.

 Use this SmartIcon from Palette 1 to print your worksheets.

Printing Options

In the steps above, you learned how to use the /Print Printer Align Go command to do a quick print—a procedure that accepts 1-2-3's default values. In fact, you are offered a variety of options when working with the Print menu subcommands. Table 16.1 gives you a look at these.

Need a Break? A page break, that is! You can add one. First, decide which row gets the page break; put the cell pointer in column A of that row, and then select the Page command from the Worksheet menu. The break appears at your chosen location.

Table 16.1 Print menu commands.

Command	Allows You To
Range	Give the range to be printed.
Line	Adjust the paper's position, line by line.
Page	Move to the top of the next page.
Options	Choose different print settings and enhancements.
Clear	Remove any previous settings.
Align	Specify the present position of the paper as the page top (dot-matrix printers only).
Go	Start printing.
Quit	Exit the Print menu.

Stop! Press Ctrl+Break to interrupt the printing process whenever necessary.

Printing Your Screen

You may need a printout of the current screen, perhaps for reference as you're developing another worksheet. Just display on-screen the part of the worksheet you want to print, and then press your Print Screen key. (Depending on your keyboard, you may or may not have to use Shift as a booster key.)

Printing in Landscape Mode

In addition to printing in *portrait mode* (across the width of the paper), Wysiwyg prints in *landscape mode* (along the length of the paper, as in Figure 16.1)—provided this mode is available on your printer. If it is not, 1-2-3 will display an error message when you select the :Print Go command. The path to follow is `:Print Config Orientation Landscape`. See Figure 16.1 for the Landscape Orientation dialog box.

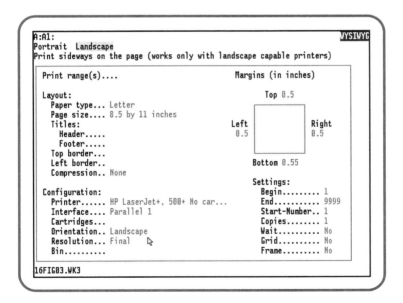

Figure 16.1 The landscape orientation for printing.

Headers and Footers

When your worksheet prints out, six lines are provided automatically for headers and footers. Three of these (at the top of the page) are reserved for the header; three more at the bottom accommodate the footer. It's very easy to enter a header or footer. Here are the steps:

1. Press / (slash) to call up the Main menu.

2. Choose Print.

3. Select Printer.

4. Choose Range; type in the range you want to print.

5. Select Options.

6. Select Header or Footer.

7. Type in, at the prompt, the text you want to appear in your header or footer (e.g., the name of your company).

8. Press Enter.

9. Choose Quit once you've entered the text. The new headers and footers are stored with your worksheet, and will print.

Optional characters are also available that will put alignment information, page numbers, and dates in headers and footers, as shown in Table 16.2.

Table 16.2 Optional characters used in headers and footers.

Character	What It Does
|	Centers any text that follows.
||	Right-justifies any text that follows
#	Prints page number at the position of the character.
@	Uses the format DD-MM-YY to print the system date.

Printing Worksheet Formulas

There may be times when you want a hard copy of the formulas in a worksheet, or need to share them with friends and colleagues.

Follow these steps to print the formulas contained in a worksheet:

1. Press / (slash) to call up the Main menu.

2. Choose Print.

3. Choose Printer.

4. Select Options.

5. Select Other.

6. Select Cell-Formulas; this specifies that only the formulas are to be printed.

91

7. Press Esc.

8. Select Range.

9. Type in the print range.

10. Choose Align.

11. Choose Go to print the range you've typed in. A list of cells appears, listing cell address, format, width, and cell contents for each one.

12. Choose Quit; 1-2-3 returns to READY mode.

In this lesson, you learned how to print either a whole worksheet or a screen, use landscape mode, and print headers, footers, and formulas. In the next lesson, you will learn how to graph your worksheet data.

Lesson 17

Graphing in Lotus 1-2-3

The next three lessons are dedicated to the art of creating, naming, saving, enhancing, and printing graphs. In this lesson, you will learn the basics: creating good-looking bar and pie graphs quickly.

Graphing Basics

You've undoubtedly heard the saying that a picture is worth a thousand words. Few people would argue the benefits of interpreting numbers by viewing graphs, as opposed to deciphering a worksheet full of numbers. Graphs show us many things about the numbers you've crunched on a worksheet. They show comparisons, trends, percentage of a whole, and progress. Some graph terms include:

X-axis   The left to right (horizontal) directions on a graph, usually indicating time line.

Y-axis   The bottom to top (vertical) direction on a graph, usually indicating value increment.

Legend   A separate box to the side of a graph that identifies the source of the x-axis data.

93

1-2-3 gives you the ability to create seven types of graphs (see Table 17.1), some familiar, some not. Yet, once you've built one type of graph, you'll see that the steps are quite similar for all types.

Table 17.1 Graph types in 1-2-3.

Type	Used For Explaining
Bar	Values in two or more ranges of data. You could use a bar graph to show average grades of five classes over a semester.
Line	Trends of data, tracked over time (e.g., the grades of five students over a semester).
Pie	How values in a series compare to a whole (e.g., the percentage of A's, B's, and C's on an exam).
Stacked Bar	The role of each data item in a total. One bar might give a percentage of all student class attendance; bar segments might show the attendance percentage of each class.
XY	Relationships between different types of numbers (e.g., total student grades compared with grades of one particular class). XY graphs are also called *scattergrams.*
HLCO	Changes in one set of data over a specified period of time (e.g., the stock market over one day).
Mixed	Two different types of data in a single graph. Often a bar graph and a line graph within one boundary.

Bar Graphs

This lesson will be easier to understand if you build a small worksheet first, and use it as an example. You could create a simple worksheet, showing average classroom test scores for two groups of students, the Bluebirds and the Redbirds. Bluebird scores are: 87, 98, and 95. Redbird scores are 78, 88, and 96 (see Figure 17.1).

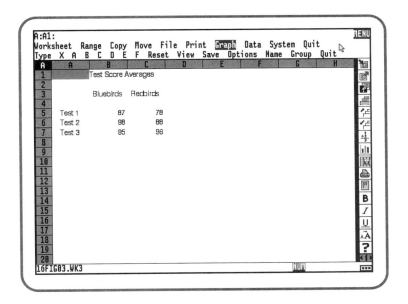

Figure 17.1 The Student Scores worksheet, with the graph command highlighted.

Using this example, you could produce a bar graph that shows how each of the two groups in the Super Student School scores on the series of first-semester tests. Once you're ready to build a graph, here are the steps to follow:

1. Press / (slash) to call up the Main menu.

95

2. Choose Graph.

3. Choose Type.

4. Select Bar as your graph type (see Figure 17.2).

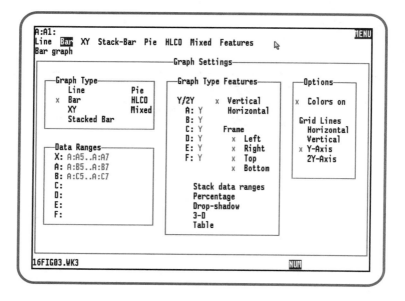

Figure 17.2   The Student graph example, with the bar graph selection highlighted.

5. Choose A as the first data range you will graph.

6. At the Enter first data range: prompt, highlight (or type in) the range; for the example, use B5..B7.

7. Select B as the second data range you will graph.

8. Select or type in the range (C5..C7 for the example).

9. Choose X.

10. Select or type in the range (`A5..A7` for the example) to tell 1-2-3 which cells to use as labels along the x-axis of the graph (`Test1`, `Test2`, `Test3` in this case).

11. Select View to see the graph you've created (see Figure 17.3).

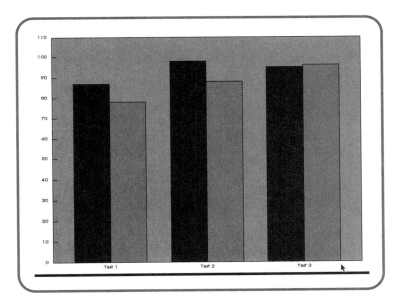

Figure 17.3 The bar graph created from the sample worksheet.

 Select the range you want to graph, and then choose this SmartIcon from palette 1 to create a quick bar graph.

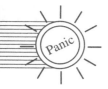

Where's the Graph? Your PC's memory (or the type of display you have) may not allow you to see your graph when you are using **WYSIWYG** mode. If this happens, return to the Main menu (Alt+F10), select Add-In Remove WYSIWYG, then repeat the steps to view your graph.

Pie Graphs

Creating a sample pie graph is simple; use the /Graph Type command, and then choose Pie. Then just specify the A range (**B5..B7** from the example) and an X range (**A5..A7** from the example). Remember, pie charts are used to depict just one set of data.

In this lesson, you learned the types of graphs 1-2-3 will allow you to set up. Then you learned how to create a bar and pie graph. The next lesson shows you how to dress up your graphs by adding enhancements. Then you will learn how to name and save your graphs.

Lesson 18
Enhancing Graphs

In this lesson, you'll learn how to give your graphs proper titles, legends, and names. You'll learn how to save your graphs, and to do something called "what-if" graphing!

Graph Enhancements?

Enhancements are "extras" you can use to make your graph special. For example, you can:

- Add titles and subtitles.

- Add and customize a legend.

- Create a background pattern.

Give Your Graph Titles

A *title* helps the reader understand the graph's purpose. Use the bar graph you created in Lesson 17 to try the following example:

Before You Add a Title Make sure to reset the Graph Type to Bar if you are using this example.

1. Press / (slash) to call up the Main menu.

2. Choose Graph.

3. Choose Options.

4. Choose Titles; 1-2-3 gives you the option of selecting titles for the first and second lines, x- and y-axis.

5. Select First. The `Enter first line of graph title:` prompt appears.

6. Type your title's first line (`Test Score Averages`, in the example graph), and press Enter.

7. Once the `Titles` command is highlighted, press Enter again.

8. Select Second.

9. Type your title's second line (`First Semester`, in the example graph), and press Enter.

10. Press F10 to display the graph (see Figure 18.1).

11. Press Esc repeatedly to return to the spreadsheet.

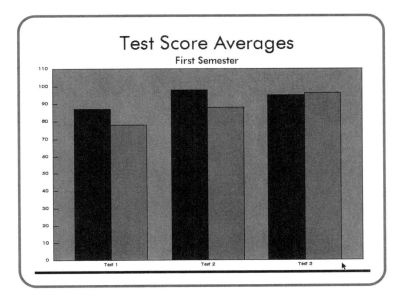

Figure 18.1   Adding titles to the sample graph.

Adding a Legend to the Graph

Legends help explain your graph's data by defining your data series. Here's how to add a legend:

1. Press / (slash) to call up the Main menu.

2. Choose Graph.

3. Choose Options.

4. Choose Legend.

5. Choose A. The `Enter legend for first data range:` prompt appears.

101

6. At the prompt, type \ (backslash) and then the address of the cell containing the label that starts your first data range (**B3** in the example).

7. Press Enter.

8. To add legends for other data ranges, repeat steps 3 through 5 for each one you want to add.

9. Press F10 to view your graph, complete with titles and legend. Press Esc to return to the worksheet.

All Together Now   Use the Graph Legends & Titles dialog box to enter all your graph's titles, legends, and data labels at once. Using the /Graph Options command will access this dialog box (see Figure 18.2).

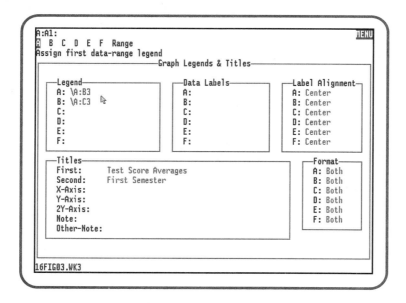

Figure 18.2   The Graph Legends & Titles dialog box.

Setting the Graph's Background Grid

You can customize your graph further by following these steps to setting a *background grid*. The grid adds texture to the graph and livens up a boring chart. Follow these steps:

1. Press / (slash) to call up the Main menu.

2. Choose Graph.

3. Choose Options.

4. Select Grid. You will be shown five more options from which to choose.

5. Select one option: Horizontal, Vertical, Both, Clear, or Y-axis. Press Enter.

6. To view the graph, press F10. 1-2-3 adds a grid to the back of your graph, as shown in Figure 18.3.

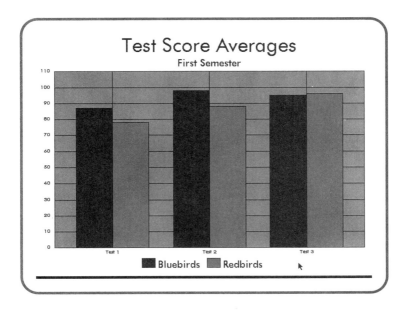

Figure 18.3   Adding a horizontal background grid.

103

Name That Graph!

You might create several graphs to accompany one worksheet. Using several graphs allows you to choose the most effective way to display the data you've crunched. When working with several graphs, you can keep them straight by naming them. Here is how to name the graph:

1. Press / (slash) to call up the Main menu.

2. Choose Graph.

3. Choose Name.

4. Choose Create.

5. Type the graph name and press Enter. 1-2-3 names the graph.

6. Press the Esc key until you return to the worksheet.

Saving Your Graph

Using the /Graph Save command when you save your worksheet will ensure that your graph is saved with the worksheet. If you want, you can use the graph by itself (for example, in the PrintGraph program). You can also save a graph independent of the worksheet. To do this, follow these steps:

1. Press / (slash) to call up the Main menu.

2. Select Graph.

3. Select Save.

4. At the `Enter graph file name:` prompt, type a name for the file.

5. Press Enter and 1-2-3 saves the file. From here, you can access the PrintGraph program to print the graph if you want.

6. Press the Esc key until you return to the worksheet.

What-If Graphing

You might want to use projected data in your worksheet, rather than actual data. Perhaps you look at a forecast and decide to increase a figure (such as projected sales income). To do this kind of *what-if graphing*, you could try out different scenarios, and see the changing results in your graph immediately. Using the command /Worksheet Window Graph lets you view the current graph alongside the worksheet data on which the graph is based. Change a figure in the worksheet, and you will see the change take effect in the graph.

In this lesson, you learned how to enhance your graph by assigning titles, legends, and names. You also learned how to save a graph, independent of the source worksheet, and were introduced to what-if graphing. In the next lesson, you will learn how to print your current and named graphs.

Lesson 19

Printing Your Graphs

In this lesson, you will learn how to print your current graph, print a named graph, and print a graph along with worksheet data.

Printing a Current Graph

If you've developed your current graph to your satisfaction, here's how to print it.

Not Ready If you are viewing the graph, press any key to return to the READY mode before you start this procedure.

1. Select Printer from the Print menu.

2. Select Align; this informs 1-2-3 that the paper is positioned at the top of the page.

3. Select Image, and then choose Current.

4. Choose Go to start printing.

Printing a Named Graph

If the graph is named, you can print it without first making it the current one. Follow these steps:

1. From the Print menu, select Printer.

2. Choose Image.

3. Select Named-Graph (see Figure 19.1).

4. Highlight the graph's name.

5. Press Enter.

6. Choose Go to start printing.

7. Choose Page; this moves the paper to the top of the next page.

8. Select Quit to return to READY mode.

Printing a Graph with Worksheet Data

Here's a chance to make a dramatic presentation! Print your graph (either current or named) with your worksheet data, on the same page.

The following steps will print your graph on the same page as your worksheet data. 1-2-3 prints the range of data. Data will print first, followed by the graph. (You can reorder the steps to print the graph first, if you want.)

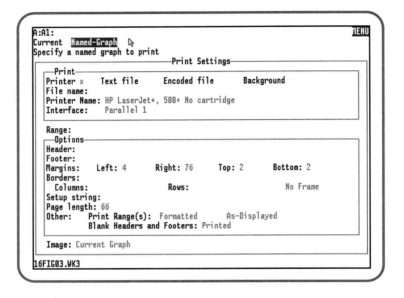

Figure 19.1   Selecting the Named-Graph option.

Printing the Worksheet Data

1. Select Printer from the Print menu.

2. Choose Range.

3. Move the cell pointer to the top of the range.

4. Press . (period) to anchor the cell pointer.

5. Highlight the whole range you intend to print.

6. Press Enter to mark the end of the range.

7. Choose Go to start printing.

Printing the Graph

1. Select Printer from the Print menu.

2. Choose Image to specify printing your graph.

3. Select Named-Graph to indicate a named graph.

4. Highlight the name of your designated graph.

5. Press Enter.

6. Choose Go to start printing your graph on the same page as the worksheet data.

7. Select Page; the paper moves to the top of the next page.

8. Select Quit to return to READY mode.

In this lesson, you learned how to print the current or named graph, and how to print a graph along with the worksheet data. In the next lesson, you will learn how to work with multiple worksheets.

Lesson 20

Working with Multiple Worksheets

In this lesson, you will learn how to work with multiple worksheets contained in one file.

Putting multiple worksheets in one file is easy and useful. Suppose, for example, you have a group of pizza parlors. You will need a file that provides an inventory of ingredients for each restaurant in the chain. But you don't want to have to switch files to get at the inventories—that means multiple worksheets in the same file.

Once you've created this convenient working arrangement, you can take advantage of these capabilities:

- Adding more worksheets to the same file.

- Copying data to a worksheet from another one in the file.

- Moving among your worksheets without leaving the file.

The first step in working with multiple worksheets is to clear all active files from your screen (if they're important, save them first!), and replace them with one blank worksheet. To accomplish this, follow these steps:

1. Call up the Worksheet submenu.

2. Select Erase.

3. Select Yes to clear all files from your screen, and remove them from your computer's working memory.

4. Retrieve your first worksheet.

Your file is now called a *single-sheet file* because there is only one worksheet in it, but that is about to change.

Add New Worksheets

Suppose you wanted to add a projected inventory for the ingredients needed to add new menu items for a second and third pizza parlor. When you have more than one worksheet in memory, you can work with any of them—or with several at once—and move from one to another as if they were actual paper stacked on your desk. When you add the new worksheets, your file becomes a *multiple-sheet file*.

The number of worksheets you can hold in one file depends on how much memory your computer has. The letters Lotus 1-2-3 uses to designate worksheets run from A through IV, but let's start with one. You'll need to be able to view both worksheets at the same time; to make this possible, change your screen display by following these steps:

1. Press / (slash) to call up the Main menu.

2. Choose Worksheet from the Main menu.

3. Choose Window from the Worksheet submenu.

111

4. Select Perspective. This option stacks the worksheets so you can see there are more than one.

Even without the new worksheets, this *perspective view* displays the spaces they will occupy (see Figure 20.1).

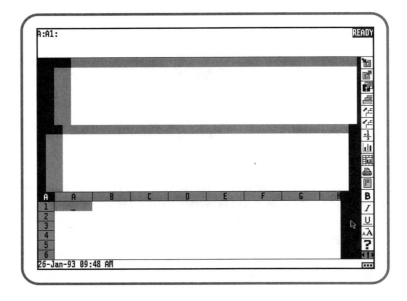

Figure 20.1 The perspective view, with space reserved for additional worksheets.

You can insert new worksheets into your file in the order you choose—preceding or following the current worksheet (the one the cell pointer occupies). Here's how:

1. Press / (slash) to call up the Main menu.

2. Select Worksheet from the Main menu.

3. Select Insert from the Worksheet submenu.

4. Choose Sheet.

5. Choose After.

6. Type in 2 to insert two worksheets after the current one.

Your file now contains three worksheets; 1-2-3 designates the original worksheet as (A), the second one as (B), and the third one as (C). Notice, however, that this process has made the original no longer current; the cell pointer moves to the first worksheet inserted after the original (worksheet B is now the current one).

Copying Between Worksheets in the Same File

Once you have multiple worksheets in place, you can use your main worksheet (**w**orksheet A) as a template or model, copying formulas and labels from it to others. Begin this procedure by specifying a three-dimensional range (*3-D range*) to copy TO. A 3-D range spans two or more consecutive worksheets in the same file, as if you were X-raying a stack of worksheets. Follow these steps:

1. Press / (slash) to call up the Main menu.

2. Select Copy.

3. Move the cell pointer to highlight worksheet A's contents.

4. To designate this range as the range to copy FROM, press Enter.

Remember: for the TO range, you need only specify the upper left cell; for a 3-D range, specify only the upper left cell of *each worksheet in the range.*

113

5. Press Ctrl+PgUp; the cell pointer moves to B:A1.

6. Press . (period); the cell pointer is anchored in B:A1.

7. Press Ctrl+PgUp; B:A1..C:A1 is highlighted.

8. To designate B:A1..C:A1 as the range to copy TO, press Enter.

Moving Between Worksheets in the Same File

Several different key combinations will enable you to move swiftly back and forth between worksheets in your multiple-sheet file.

- Ctrl+PgDn takes you to worksheet A.

- Ctrl+PgUp takes you to worksheet B. The cell pointer moves to the cell you highlighted the last time that worksheet was active. You can use F5 (the GoTo key) to move between worksheets, and to zero in on specific cells.

- Ctrl+Home takes you to A:A1.

In this lesson, you learned how to work with multiple worksheets. In the next lesson, you will learn how to create a database in Lotus 1-2-3.

Lesson 21

Building a Lotus 1-2-3 Database

In this lesson, you will learn how to create a database in Lotus 1-2-3.

Database Concepts

If you're new to working with databases, here are some basic terms:

- **Database**   A collection of facts and figures, perhaps relating to inventory, personnel, customers, or your softball league.

- **Fields**   An area where you enter information such as name, age, birthday, or quantity.

- **Record**   A collection of all the facts and figures relating to one person or thing which are entered into fields. (You can have a record for each employee or a record for each team member.)

- **Sort**   Arranging records in numerical or alphabetical order.

115

While 1-2-3 is a spreadsheet program, and not a specialized database program, you can use it to create a simple database. Storing and retrieving a number of important items (e.g., clients' names, addresses, and phone numbers) can come in handy.

How the Database Works

Lotus 1-2-3's database looks (as you might expect) just like a worksheet: rows stand for records, columns stand for fields. A simple database is shown in Figure 21.1.

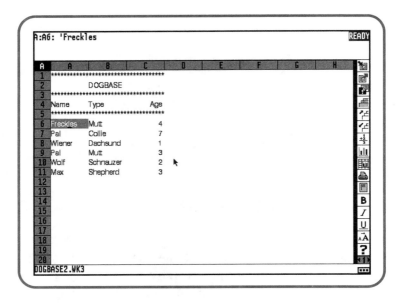

Figure 21.1   A simple 1-2-3 database, where the rows are records and the columns are fields.

Building Your Database

It is easy to build a 1-2-3 database. First, plan. Think about the type of information you will need and in what order it should appear. Write this information down on paper before you enter your database into 1-2-3.

Entering Labels

Enter a label (field) by typing the label you want to use, and pressing → to move to the next cell. Repeat this step until you've entered all your labels for all the fields in your database.

A Mixed Bag! Some entries contain a mix of letters and numbers. If you want an entry formatted as text so it won't be used in a calculation (e.g., phone numbers), precede the entry with an apostrophe ('). This tells 1-2-3 that the entry is a label rather than a value.

Entering and Saving Data

Once you have established the basic organization of your database, it's time to enter your records. Type the data into each cell (and then press Enter), as displayed in Figure 21.1.

Saving your database is similar to saving any other spreadsheet file. Use /File Save and name the database.

In this lesson, you learned basic database concepts and a method for using 1-2-3 to build a database. In the next lesson, you will learn how to sort records.

Lesson 22

Sorting Your Database

In this lesson, you will learn how to sort the data in your database.

Understanding Sorting

Data in a database begs to be organized, sorted, and re-trieved! Suppose you have 200 records—for example, names and addresses of 200 friends and family. A way of alphabetizing these names would be useful; then you need only scroll through your list to locate a particular record.

Lotus 1-2-3 allows you to choose how to do the sort by letting you designate a specific field as a "key." This *key field* can be a Lastname field, City field, or Zip field. You can use any of the fields in your database as a key field; in fact, you can use two key fields in the same sort.

For example, in a *two-key sort*, you can first sort on the Lastname field (as the primary field), and then sort on the Firstname field (as the secondary field). If you sort alphabetically on full names—and have two Joneses (a Jim Jones and a Tim Jones)—Jim's name will appear on the sorted list before Tim's name.

Key Fields Use *key fields* to designate the kind of sort operation you want to do. To sort all the records in your database alphabetically by city, for example, use the City field as the key field.

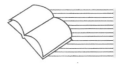

Using One Key Field for Sorting

For working through the steps in this lesson and in Lesson 23, construct the small database shown in Figure 22.1

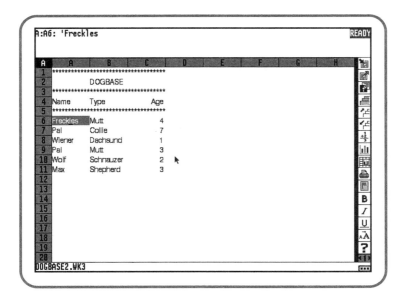

Figure 22.1   A sample unsorted database.

For this example, begin by making sure the database portion of the worksheet is on-screen (see Figure 22.1). Then alphabetize the dog records according to Name. Here are the steps for sorting these records:

119

1. From the Data menu, choose Sort.

2. Choose Data-Range.

3. At the Enter data range: prompt, type in the cell addresses of the range to be sorted (or use the mouse to highlight them). Type or select only the data range to be sorted; omit the labels from this step. (For example, in this database, highlight cells A6..C11.)

4. Press Enter.

5. Select Primary-Key to choose the key field.

6. Move the cell pointer to an entry in your chosen key field. (For example, in this database, move your pointer to cell A6 and press Enter.)

7. Type A if you want to choose Ascending order, or D to choose Descending order. (In this example, select A.)

8. Press Enter.

9. Select Go. 1-2-3 will sort the database according to your settings. (The example alphabetizes dog names. In the next section, you'll see how to use a secondary sort to group the dogs named Pal.)

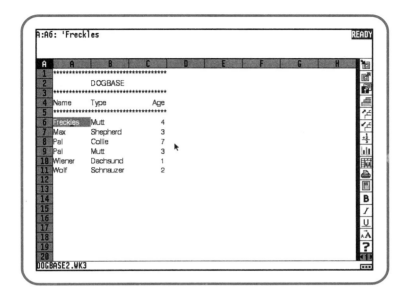

Figure 22.2 The database has been sorted by the dogs' names.

Using Two Key Fields for Sorting

You've read in the preceding section of this lesson that 1-2-3 can sort on more than one key field. Try this example to sort on two key fields.

1. From the Data menu, select Sort.

2. Choose Data-Range.

3. At the Enter data range prompt, type in the cell addresses of the range to be sorted (or use the mouse to highlight them). Type or select only the data range to be sorted; omit the labels from this step. (In the example, type A6..C11.)

121

4. Press Enter.

5. Select Primary-Key to begin choosing the first key field.

6. When you've decided on a field to serve as first key field, move the cell pointer to one of its entries. (In this example, move the cell pointer to cell A6.)

7. Press Enter.

8. Select Ascending or Descending order, and press Enter (in this example, select A).

9. Select the Secondary-Key to begin choosing the second key field.

10. Decide on a second key field; move the cell pointer to one of its entries (in the example, choose B6). Press Enter.

11. Indicate the sort order (in this example, select A).

12. Return to the Sort menu option and select Go. 1-2-3 uses your two key fields to sort the records (see Figure 22.3). Notice that the dogs named Pal are now sorted by their ages.

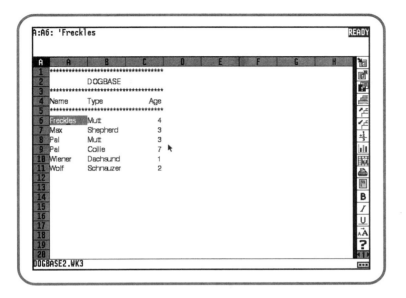

Figure 22.3 The result of the two-key sort.

In this lesson, you learned how to sort the records in your database, using one and two key fields. In the final lesson, you will learn how to search for specific records.

Lesson 23

Querying Your Database

In this lesson, you will learn how to search a database for a specific record.

How Queries Work

The capability of looking for specific records in a database is the chief reason databases are built. For example, if you have a big list of names and addresses, finding all records that fall within a certain Zip code designation can be handy.

Here are some database terms you'll need to understand, in order to work with 1-2-3's search options:

- **Data query**   Specifies a record or a group of records for the database to find, and asks it to start looking.

- **Criteria range**   The conditions you impose on the search, so that 1-2-3 knows which records to look for.

- **Output range**   The cell range that will hold the records 1-2-3 extracts or copies from your database.

The Criteria Range

You can use the dog-based database that you built in the last lesson to work through this lesson. You may want to find all the mutts, for example—all the records that show Mutt entered in the Type field. First, specify a *criteria range* so that 1-2-3 knows what conditions its findings have to meet. Follow these steps to create a criteria range:

1. Move the pointer to some place on the worksheet other than the database (in this example, use A17).

2. Type CRITERIA RANGE, and then press →.

3. Type the name of the field for which you want 1-2-3 to search (in this example, Type).

4. Press →.

5. Type in the specific information you want 1-2-3 to find in your designated field (for this example, type Mutt and press →. Your criteria range should look like the range in Figure 23.1.

6. Select /Data Query. The Query Settings menu appears.

7. Type I; the Input range: prompt appears.

8. At the prompt, type the cell addresses of the records you want to include in the search, or use the mouse to point to them. You can specify the entire database. (In this example, choose A4..C11 to include the field names and all data, and press Enter.)

9. Select Criteria.

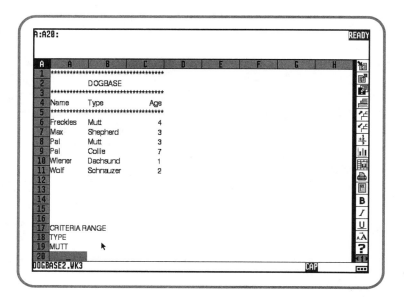

```
A:A20:                                                    READY

A      A        B        C       D      E      F      G      H
1  ********************************
2             DOGBASE
3  ********************************
4  Name      Type            Age
5  ********************************
6  Freckles  Mutt             4
7  Max       Shepherd         3
8  Pal       Mutt             3
9  Pal       Collie           7
10 Wiener    Dachsund         1
11 Wolf      Schnauzer        2
12
13
14
15
16
17 CRITERIA RANGE
18 TYPE
19 MUTT
20
DOGBASE2.WK3                                           CAP
```

Figure 23.1   A criteria range designated for a search.

10. Type the name of the range that contains the criteria field's name and data (in this example, type in A18..A19); press Enter.

11. Choose /Find. 1-2-3 locates the first record that meets the conditions of your criteria range (see Figure 23.2).

Find Next   To find additional records, press → to move to the next record that meets the search criteria. Press Esc to end the search.

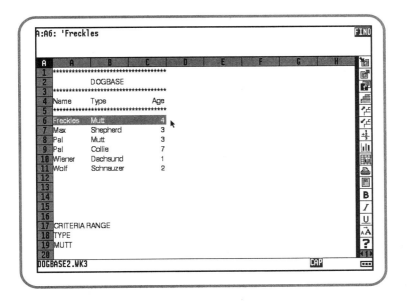

Figure 23.2   Locating records in the criteria range.

Extracting Records from the Database

It's possible to copy a group of records from your database, and place the copy in another range on the worksheet. The process is called _extracting_ records; to do it, follow these steps:

1. Use /Copy to copy the field names of the records you want to extract (such as E4..G4) to a new location on the worksheet.

2. As you did for the /Data Query Find, select the criteria range.

127

3. Scroll through the records found using →. When completed, press Esc.

4. Select Output and indicate the range of field names you copied (in this example, E4..G4).

5. Select Extract and 1-2-3 copies all records that meet the conditions of the criteria range, and places them in the output range (see Figure 23.3).

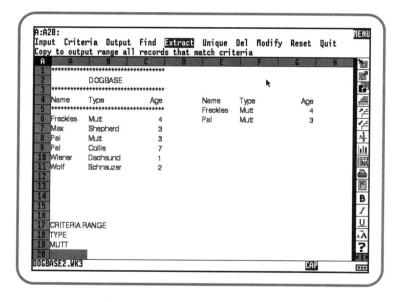

Figure 23.3 Extracted copies are recorded into the output range.

In this lesson, you learned the basics of querying your 1-2-3 database.

This lesson concludes the *10 Minute Guide to Lotus 1-2-3 Release 3.4*. Following this lesson, you will find helpful materials in the "Overtime" section. Best wishes as you work with this software.

Overtime

Appendix A
SmartIcons

Icon	Palette	Enables You To
	1	Save your worksheet to a disk.
	1	Retrieve a worksheet file from disk.
	1	Read a file into memory after the current file.
	1	See three worksheets, stacked up.
	1	Move to the worksheet after this one.
	1	Move to the worksheet before this one.
	1	Calculate the sum of values in a range.
	1	Create, edit, or display a graph.
	1	Add your graph to the worksheet.
	1	Print a selected range of cells.
	1	Print the previous (or a specified) range.

131

Icon	Palette	Enables You To
B	1	Add boldface to (or remove it from) a range.
I	1	Add italics to (or clear them from) a range.
<u>U</u>	1	Add single underlining to (or remove it from) data in a range.
ₐ→A	1	Cycle through available fonts for a range.
?	1	Start the Help system.
U (double underline)	2	Add double underlining to data in a range, or remove it.
$	2	Format values in a range as currency, or restore global format.
0,0	2	Format values in a range using comma format, or restore global format.
%	2	Format values in a range using percent format, or restore global format.
(left-align icon)	2	Left-align a range's labels.
(center icon)	2	Center a range's labels.
(right-align icon)	2	Right-align a range's labels.
(insert rows icon)	3	Insert one or more rows above the highlighted rows.
(insert columns icon)	3	Insert one or more columns to the left of the highlighted column.
(delete rows icon)	3	Delete all rows in the highlighted range.

Icon	Palette	Enables You To
	3	Delete all columns in the highlighted range.
	3	Sort a database in ascending order; current column is the sort key.
	3	Sort a database in descending order; current column is the sort key.
	4	Move cell pointer left one cell.
	4	Move cell pointer right one cell.
	4	Move cell pointer up one cell.
	4	Move cell pointer down one cell.
	4	Move cell pointer to upper left corner of worksheet.
	4	Move cell pointer to lower right corner of worksheet.
	5	Move cell pointer to a cell you specify.
	5	Find or replace characters in a range's labels and formulas.
	5	Copy highlighted range to a range you specify.
	5	Move highlighted range to a range you specify.
	5	Cancel previous action or command if Undo feature is on.
	5	Erase highlighted range.
	6	Display current graph.

133

Icon	Palette	Enables You To
	7	Select and run a macro.
	7	Add an icon to your custom palette.
	7	Remove an icon from your custom palette.
	7	Rearrange icons on custom palettes.

Popular Lotus 1-2-3 Functions

This table lists the functions used most commonly in Lotus 1-2-3 Release 3.4. *Date-number* means the set of values representing the date; *time-number* means the set of values representing the time.

Function	Calculates/Returns
@DATE	Date-number (year, month, and day).
@DAY	Day of the month (in date-number).
@MONTH	Month (in date-number).
@YEAR	Year (in date-number).
@HOUR	Hour (in time-number).
@MINUTE	Minutes (in time-number).
@SECOND	Seconds (in time-number).
@TIME	Complete time-number (hours, minutes, and seconds).
@NOW	The current date and time on your PC's clock.
@TODAY	The current date on your PC's clock (date-number).

Function	Calculates/Returns
@ABS	An absolute (positive) numerical value.
@INT	The integer portion of a value.
@RAND	Random value between 0 and 1.
@ROUND	A value rounded to a specified number of decimal places.
@CELL	Information about a cell, its contents, or its settings.
@COLS	The total columns in a range.
@ROWS	The total rows in a range.
@AVG	The average of a list of values.
@COUNT	In a list of ranges, the number of cells containing data.
@MAX	In a list of values, the largest value.
@MIN	In a list of values, the smallest value.
@STD	For a list of values, the population standard deviation.
@SUM	The total of a list of values.

Appendix C
DOS Primer

This section highlights some of the DOS procedures you will use during your work with Lotus 1-2-3 Release 3.4.

Preparing Disks

The first step in preparing disks for storing programs and data is formatting the disks.

What Is Formatting? The *formatting* procedure writes important information on the disk, preparing it to store data. You can't place any information— programs or data of any kind—on a new disk before the disk is formatted. Formatting also erases any information on a previously used diskette. Do not format your hard disk drive, however, because formatting a hard disk erases all your programs along with the information on the hard disk.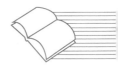

1. Turn the computer on.

2. If the system asks you for the date and time, type these in, and press Enter after each entry. (Not all systems ask

for the date and time.) Enter the date in the form MM:DD:YY (such as `02:25:93`) and the time in the form HH:MM:SS (such as `5:45:00`).

3. When the DOS prompt is displayed (it will be shown as C>, D>, or A>, depending on the type of system you have and how it is set up), insert the first blank disk into drive A or B, and close the drive door.

4. Type the name of the drive where you inserted the blank disk, following the name with a colon (`A:` or `B:`, for example). Then press Enter.

5. Type `FORMAT A:` or `FORMAT B:` and press Enter. The system will tell you to insert the disk (which you've already done).

6. Press Enter. The system begins formatting the disk. When the format is complete, the system asks whether you want to format another.

7. If you want to format additional disks, type `Y` and repeat these steps.

A good (and useful) example of formatting is making a backup copy of your Lotus 1-2-3 program. Repeat these steps as many times as necessary to format the *backup disks* for your Lotus 1-2-3 program. Now you're ready to make the copy.

Making a Backup Copy of 1-2-3

To make a backup copy of your Lotus 1-2-3 program follow these steps:

Your Own Backup Copy   Consult your Lotus 1-2-3 user's manual to double-check which disks to copy first—and remember, it's strictly for your own use as a registered user, to save wear and tear on the original disks.

1. Place the first original program disk in drive A.

2. In drive B, place the blank, formatted disk onto which you're going to copy the program disk.

3. Type DISKCOPY A:B: and press Enter. (If you have two drives that are different sizes—such as one 5.25-inch and one 3.5-inch drive—or you have only one floppy drive, use DISKCOPY A:A: instead.)

   The system then copies to drive B the information from the disk in drive A. When the operation is complete, the system asks whether you want to copy another disk.

4. Type Y. Repeat the DISKCOPY procedure until you've copied all your Lotus 1-2-3 disks. Now you're ready to install the program. (See the inside front cover of this book for installation instructions.)

DOS Confusion   If you're having trouble understanding some of these commands, don't worry—the formatting and copying procedures are part of DOS, your computer's operating system. For more information about using DOS, see *The First Book of DOS* from Alpha Books.

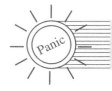

139

Working with Directories

DOS enables you to organize your files in *directories* and *subdirectories*. You can think of this organization as a "tree" structure—each directory can have subdirectories (like the branches splitting off from the trunk of a tree).

Making Directories

To create a directory, you use the MD (Make Directory) command. Follow these steps:

1. At the DOS prompt, type **MD** *directoryname*. (Substitute the name of the directory you are creating in place of *directoryname*.)

2. Press Enter.

This command causes DOS to create the directory under the name you specified, and place the new directory in the root directory.

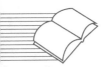

Roots, Continued The *root directory* is the main directory on your disk (the "trunk" of the "tree"). All other directories and subdirectories are divisions of the root directory.

During installation, Lotus 1-2-3 will create a 1-2-3 directory for you. You may want, however, to create additional directories for storing your data files.

Moving to a Directory

You need to be able to move from one directory to another. To change directories, you use the CD (Change Directory) command:

1. At the DOS prompt, type CD*directoryname*. In this *command line*, the backslash (\\) tells DOS to begin at the root directory and move to the directory you specified under the root. You use the backslash to separate all directories and subdirectories in a command line. For example, if you wanted to move to a subdirectory of a directory, the command line would look like this:

   CD*directoryname**subdirectoryname*

2. Press Enter. DOS moves to the directory or subdirectory you specified.

Displaying a Directory's Contents

To see which files are stored in a directory, you use the DIR (Directory) command:

1. Change to the directory you want to display.

2. Type DIR.

3. Press Enter. DOS displays a list of all the files in the current directory.

Working with Files

DOS also includes commands you can use to work with the files you create. This section briefly introduces the procedures for copying, deleting, and renaming files.

Copying Files

When you want to copy files using DOS, you use the COPY command:

1. Move to the directory that stores the file(s) you want to copy.

2. Type COPY *filename1 filename2*. In this command line, *filename1* is the name of the existing file you want to copy, and *filename2* is the new name you want to give to the copy of the file.

   You can also copy a file to a different directory by typing
   COPY *filename1drivename\directoryname\filename*, making the appropriate substitutions.

3. Press Enter.

Deleting Files

When you delete files using DOS, you use the ERASE (or DEL) command:

1. Move to the directory that stores the file(s) you want to erase.

2. Type one of these two command lines:

   ERASE *filename*

   or

   DEL *filename*

3. Press Enter.

4. When DOS asks you for confirmation, type Y. DOS then deletes the file.

Renaming Files

You use the RENAME (or REN) command to rename files in DOS:

1. Move to the directory that stores the file you want to rename.

2. Type one of these two command lines:

   RENAME *filename1 filename2*

   or

   REN *filename1 filename2*

   In these command lines, *filename1* is the name of the existing file, and *filename2* is the new name you want to assign to the file.

3. Press Enter. DOS renames the file, and keeps it in the current directory.

   For more information about using DOS commands, consult *The First Book of MS-DOS*.

Index

D